CIVIL WAR TRAILS

50 Men and Women Who Inalterably Changed the Civil War Era

Gene Schmiel

Civil War Trailblazers and Troublemakers

Copyright © 2020 by Eugene D. Schmiel

All rights reserved. No part of this publication may be reproduced, distributed, or transmitted in any form or by any means, without prior written permission

Please visit the author's web-site:
https://civilwarhistory-geneschmiel.com

Please visit the author's amazon.com web-site:
https://www.amazon.com/-/e/B00HV4SSWK

Cover Design: Gene Schmiel:

Cover Image: From top left, pictures of: Frederick Douglass; Union General Ben Butler; Clara Barton; William Tecumseh Sherman; Abraham Lincoln; Confederate General and Cherokee Indian Stand Watie; Harriet Tubman, Andrew Johnson, and Braxton Bragg. These and 40 others, as well as the collective group "50th Trailblazer" are the "change agents" in this book who had a wide-ranging effect on the Civil War era and, in most cases, American History.

Frontispiece: Photo including three trailblazers at Antietam: Lincoln, Dr. Johnathan Letterman, and General Henry Hunt.

CIVIL WAR PERSONALITIES, 50 AT A TIME SERIES:

Number One

For my family, even those who don't understand

why the Civil War is not over.

Also by Gene Schmiel

Citizen-General: Jacob Dolson Cox

Lincoln, Antietam, and a Northern Lost Cause

Ohio Heroes of the Battle of Franklin

Civil War Musings and Reflections

CIVIL WAR TRAILBLAZERS

AND TROUBLEMAKERS

Three trailblazers, Dr. Jonathan Letterman (seventh from left), General Henry Hunt (behind Lincoln), and President Abraham Lincoln, with General George McClellan at Antietam

Contents

PREFACE ix

Chapter I: *From "Beast Butler" to "Stonewall of the West"* 1

Chapter II: *Lost Causers, Heroes, and a Crusader* 41

Chapter III: *Leaders, Incompetents, and Innovators* 81

Chapter IV: *Creativity and Military Blindness* 123

Chapter V: *Uncommon Men, Women and Their Causes* 163

Chapter VI: *The 50th Trailblazer: A Collective View* 201

PREFACE

Trailblazer: pioneer, pathfinder, inventor, creator.

Troublemaker: firebrand, instigator, agitator.

War has strange bedfellows. It often brings forth the best and the worst in a society: the brave and the cowardly; the patriots and the traitors; the humanitarians and the exploiters; the leaders and those who fail at leadership; and most definitely the trailblazers and the troublemakers. The Civil War was no exception. In fact, it had more than its share of trailblazers and troublemakers, probably because it was so unexpected, so stressful, and so transformative of American society.

Trailblazers and troublemakers tend to be visionaries in the sense that they have a cause and perceive that society should be changed in some way. They ignore or avoid the path of least resistance. They innovate; they create; they instigate; and as they see opportunities either for society as a whole or for themselves, they take action. Sometimes that action is positive, sometimes it is negative, but it is always focused on change, often for the sake of change.

In this book I have described 49 individuals from the Civil War era who were in one or the other category, and sometimes both! These agents of change inalterably transformed the Civil War era and American history.

There are obviously far more than 49 people in this era who can be classified as trailblazers and/or troublemakers, but I have chosen that number as a representative sample. Inevitably, there will be those who disagree with my choices and my judgments. That is why the "re-fighting" of the Civil War persists and remains a fascinating and often bewildering part of our history.

I have presented my 49 subjects in alphabetical order for easy reference. I make absolutely no claim to originality, except in my opinions. Further, my short essays are not intended to be comprehensive. Rather, they and the related images are focused on the specific ways that these individuals belong in one or the other category – or both. Because there is a great deal more to learn about them, I have added a "Further Reading" note after each person as a starting point.

But what, the reader might ask, about the 50th person? I decided to add, in a separate chapter, a "50th trailblazer" in the form of photos of a representative group of anonymous, yet important Civil War era persons. These people: infantrymen, sailors, nurses, drummer boys, chaplains, cooks, etc. were the support staff for the major persona. They were all trailblazers, each in his or her own way. And while their history is lost, their images remain.

It is at this point in a book that the author takes full responsibility for any and all errors. I do so now, with thanks to all the others who contributed, especially the Library of Congress, whose wonderful website (loc.gov) provided almost all of the images I have used. In the spirit of accuracy and relevancy, I have presented the images mostly as they appear on the loc.gov web-site, with the flaws and imperfections inherent in the photography of the era. Thanks also to Hal Jespersen for his wonderful maps, including all of those from his excellent web-site: http://www.cwmaps.com/freemaps.html

Chapter I: *From "Beast Butler" to "Stonewall of the West"*

This first group spans the field of well-known and loved/hated people to persons in the background whose decisions and actions had a more significant impact than they might have in a less titanic time than the Civil War era.

Clara Barton's (1821-1912) work as a nurse and founder of the American Red Cross are legends in American history.

William Bate (1826-1905) performed adequately as a Confederate General, but hesitated at key points during the Battles of Spring Hill and Franklin.

Mary Ann (Mother) Bickerdyke (1817-1901) was in many ways the founder of modern American nursing.

John Wilkes Booth (1838-1865) committed one of the most heinous crimes in American history.

Matthew Brady's (1822-1896) photographs of the blood and gore of war had an enormous impact on popular understanding.

Confederate General **Braxton Bragg's** (1817-1876) cantankerous personality was a major detriment to the rebel cause.

Confederate General and former U.S. Vice President **John Breckinridge** (1821-1875) played a key role in keeping the Confederacy afloat and was a respected interlocutor with the North.

Union General **Ben Butler** (1818-1893) was one of the most hated men in the South because of his actions in New Orleans.

Confederate General **Patrick Cleburne**, (1828-1864) known as "Stonewall of the West," had his sterling war record "tarnished" for suggesting that blacks should be recruited as soldiers.

Union General **Jacob Cox** (1828-1900) was a champion of the capabilities and abilities of "Citizen-Soldiers."

Clara Barton, Angel of the Battlefield

CLARA BARTON
From portrait taken in Civil War and authorized
by her as the one she wished to be remembered by

Clara Barton and American Nursing

Like most of the hundreds of women who engaged in nursing during the Civil War, Clara Barton had neither medical training nor any hint that she would be "good" at this profession. However, acting on her own initiative, she overcame the prejudices of the age and provided vital services at a time when medical practices were barely adequate. Modern American nursing was "born" on Civil War battlefields, and Clara Barton was one of its most important parents, even though "nurse" was a title she repeatedly rejected.

Barton was a patent clerk in Washington when she had her first nursing experience, aiding Massachusetts troops attacked by a pro-secessionist mob in Baltimore in April 1861. Having seen how unprepared medical personnel were, she began to organize and gather supplies in her offices. In her memoirs, Barton emphasized that she performed this work "to get timely supplies to those needing" rather than being a "nurse."

In August 1862 Barton trailblazed a new approach to her assistance by actually going to battlefields during and after the fighting. At Cedar Mountain, Second Manassas, South Mountain, and Antietam, she brought her supplies and comfort to the troops. It was at Antietam, where she assisted men as the bullets were flying, that she gained the title, "Angel of the Battlefield."

Later, Barton worked at the Battle of Fredericksburg and during the attack on Fort Wagner in South Carolina led by the 54th Massachusetts "Colored" troops. The latter's bravery, dramatized in the movie *Glory,* brought home to Barton the importance of emancipation. She became the superintendent of an army hospital in Washington from 1864 until the end of the war.

After the war, she turned to another trailblazing effort, discovering the identity of the dead and wounded. The Union army kept few records, so Barton solicited letters from families in search of the fate of their loved ones. Barton claimed that her "Office of Missing Soldiers" identified over 20,000 men out of the nearly 200,000 reported missing and helped arrange for their proper burials.

In 1869 Barton visited Geneva, Switzerland and learned of the work of the International Red Cross. She was the founder of the American Red Cross, and was its founding president, an office she held from 1881 to 1904.

Today her legacy is memorialized at the National Park Service's "Clara Barton National Historic Site" in Glen Echo, Maryland, and the "Clara Barton's Missing Soldiers Office Museum," in Washington.

(Below is an image of the monument to Clara Barton on the Antietam battlefield, very near to where she ministered to the wounded).

Further Reading: Donald Pflanz, *Clara Barton's Civil War: Between Bullet and Hospital.* Westholme Publishing, 2018; Elizabeth Brown Pryor, *Clara Barton, Professional Angel.* University of Pennsylvania Press, 2011.

William Bate, Confederate Political General

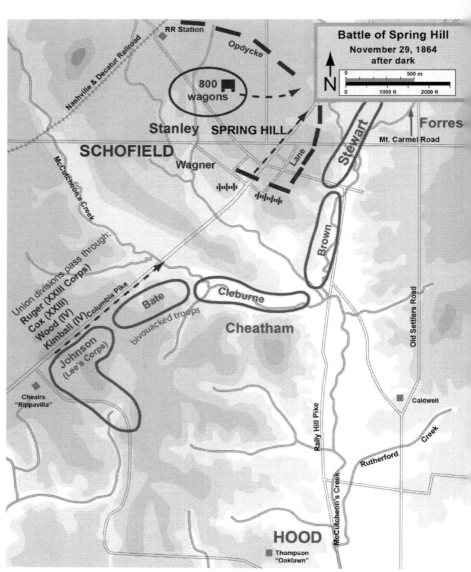

Map by Hal Jespersen, www.cwmaps.com

William Bate and the Franklin-Nashville Campaign

Working as a clerk aboard a Mississippi River steamboat, Bate made a fateful decision in 1846 -- to volunteer for the Mexican War. He later became active in Democratic politics, winning a seat in the Tennessee House at the age of 23 and becoming a district Attorney General in 1854. During the secession crisis, he supported John Breckinridge for President, and when the war began he enlisted in a Tennessee Confederate company.

Bate's first duties were to protect Virginia's railroads, and his 2nd Tennessee Infantry was in reserve at the Battle of First Bull Run, July 1861. He then asked to be transferred West, and he was placed in Albert Sidney Johnston's Army of Mississippi. Bate was seriously wounded at Shiloh. Afterward, according to legend, he became a troublemaker for the first time after he was told that one of his legs had to be amputated. While a negative reaction is understandable, his was more extreme than most: he pulled a gun and threatened the surgeon. He kept his leg, but walked with a limp the rest of his life.

Bate returned to duty under Bragg in 1863, and fought at Chickamauga and Missionary Ridge. He was promoted to Major General in early 1864. That year he was one of the Generals asked by Patrick Cleburne to consider his proposal to arm blacks to aid the Confederacy in exchange for their freedom. Bate opposed the idea. During the Atlanta campaign in August 1864 he was shot in the knee and took several weeks to recover – while keeping his leg intact this time also.

It was during the November-December 1864 Franklin-Nashville campaign that Bate caused some trouble for his commanders. Whether that was because of his new injury, it is hard to say. But at two critical battles, Spring Hill and Franklin, the usually-industrious Bate hesitated at key moments.

At Spring Hill (see above) he was supposed to move to the left flank to block Schofield's march to the north. But, blaming (for good reason) conflicting orders, he ultimately stopped short of his objective. On the night of November 29, the Union troops walked right by Bate's bivouacked forces without being touched. At Franklin the next day, Bate's men were supposed to attack the Union right, which was the most vulnerable segment of the line. Bate advanced slowly and hesitantly, and his men were unable to break the Union line while also suffering major casualties. Bate stayed with the remnants of the Army of Tennessee after the disastrous defeat at Nashville, and he surrendered along with Joe Johnston at Greensboro, North Carolina.

After the war he returned to politics, and in 1882 was elected to the first of two terms as Governor of Tennessee. He was then elected to the U.S. Senate in 1887, where he served until his death in 1905.

(Below is an image of the Battle of Franklin – Bate is at the bottom left, on the Confederate left flank, under the command of Frank Cheatham).

Further Reading: Jacobson, Eric A., and Richard A. Rupp. *For Cause & for Country: A Study of the Affair at Spring Hill and the Battle of Franklin.* Franklin, TN: O'More Publishing, 2007; Jacob Cox, *The Battle of Franklin, a Monograph*, New York: Scribner's, 1897.

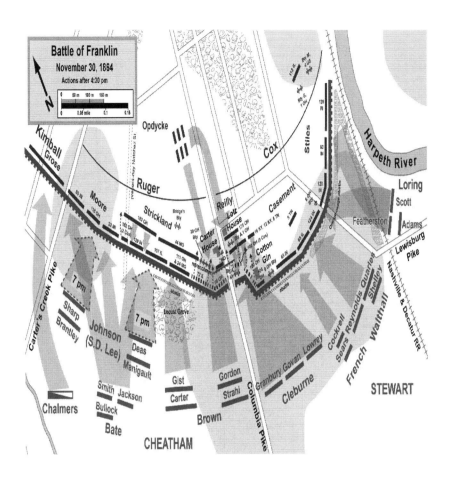

"Mother" Bickerdyke

Mary Ann Bickerdyke, Nursing Pioneer

Clara Barton is rightfully regarded as the most important nursing pioneer for the Union during the Civil War. However, no nurses were more active or effective than "Mother" Bickerdyke, so called by the Union troops because of her caring nature. A large and indomitable woman, this trailblazer in medical care was also known as the "Calico Cyclone." That reflected her inclination to storm into field hospitals like an avenging angel to begin the critical work of assisting the wounded.

Given the suspicion by men of that era of women who attempted to act in ways considered "inappropriate for a woman," it is not surprising that her abrupt style was not always appreciated. On one such occasion, a military doctor allegedly asked her on what authority she was acting. She responded, "On the authority of Lord God Almighty—have you anything that outranks that?" Eventually, with Grant and Sherman as her patrons, she outranked just about everyone else!

Her nursing career began when her church learned of the filthy conditions in field hospitals near Cairo, Illinois, in 1861. Bickerdyke was commissioned by the U.S. Sanitary Commission to go to the aid of those hospitals, and her work there soon caught Grant's attention. Eventually Grant made her his chief of nursing. Historian James McPherson notes that she was the only woman that Sherman allowed in his advanced base hospitals. By the end of the war, with the help of the Sanitary Commission, she had built some 300 hospitals and aided the wounded at 19 different battles, mainly in the West.

Her contributions were so epic that at Sherman's request, Mother Bickerdyke was given the special honor of riding at the head of the XVth corps during the Grand Review of the Armies on May 24, 1865 in Washington. (see below)

After the war she became an attorney and helped veterans to gain their rightful pensions. Bickerdyke herself was one of the few women rewarded with a pension. However, it would not be granted until 1886.

Further Reading: Nina Brown Baker, *Cyclone in Calico: The Story of Mary Ann Bickerdyke.* Boston: Little, Brown, 1952.; Larry G. Eggleston, *Women in the Civil War: Extraordinary Stories of Soldiers, Spies, Nurses, Doctors, Crusaders, and Others.* Jefferson, N.C.: McFarland, 2003..

John Wilkes Booth, Assassin

John Wilkes Booth, Worst Troublemaker of All

The story of Booth's perfidy in participating in a plot to decapitate the Union leadership needs no repeating. Nor should one forget that most Confederate leaders, including Robert E. Lee and Joseph Johnston, condemned the assassination of Lincoln. They recognized that Lincoln was on the verge of implementing a moderate Reconstruction in which most rebels would have been allowed to return to their pre-war lives unfettered.

So why did Booth commit such an atrocity? He likely had at least a touch of insanity. Like many of his fellow members of the radical group, "Knights of the Golden Circle," he believed that Union victory and emancipation would destroy Southern civilization. In his hate for abolitionism, he had made a special effort to witness John Brown's hanging. And while attending Lincoln's second inaugural address, Booth reportedly said he regretted not killing him then.

Booth reportedly believed that killing Lincoln and his entire cabinet would bring chaos to the Union government. Further, he may have thought that Lincoln's death would provide a lifeline for a Confederate victory by the sole remaining major army in the field in North Carolina, led by Joseph Johnston.

Of the several assassins in his cabal, only Booth was "successful" in killing his intended victim. The succession of Andrew Johnson to the presidency after Lincoln's death only underlined the madness of Booth's action. Lincoln the superb politician with a war victory in hand could have presided over a Reconstruction process which would have been far preferable to the one that actually ensued.

(Below is an image of the theater box at Ford's Theater where Lincoln was sitting when he was shot):

Further Reading: Michael W. Kauffman, *American Brutus: John Wilkes Booth and the Lincoln Conspiracies.* New York: Random House, 2004; Edward Steers, Jr., *Blood on the Moon: The Assassination of Abraham Lincoln.* Lexington: University Press of Kentucky. 2001..

Matthew Brady, Image Maker

Matthew Brady and the New Reality

The Civil War was a watershed not only for the military, but also for many other professions, from nursing to photography. Brady's trailblazing efforts to publicize the awful actuality of war via his "you were there" photographs were a major contribution to popular understanding.

Brady was already famous when the war began because of the prominence of his New York photographic studio. In 1849 he opened a studio in Washington and there photographed major political leaders, including presidents. Lincoln reportedly said, after having his picture taken before giving a speech at the Cooper Union in New York, "Brady and the Cooper Institute made me president" by widely publicizing his image (see below)

When the war began, Brady had an inkling that sending his photographers into the field (see below) to take "action photos" of the realities of war would be good for business. The popularity of his photos of the battlefield and people surrounding the First Battle of Bull Run convinced him to continue. It should be noted that Brady himself rarely visited the battlefields, usually sending his assistants.

Brady's photos of the aftermath of the Battle of Antietam, primarily of landmarks and dead and mangled bodies, were a turning point in popular perception. For the public, war was no longer a series of parades cheering young men going on a lark to chase away the enemy. It was a horrible reality, through which tens of thousands of those who viewed the photos in Brady's studio were then undergoing, at least vicariously. (see below)

Brady also made numerous photographs of the Battle of Gettysburg, and he and his assistants accompanied Grant during the Overland campaign in 1864-5. He was even able to convince Robert E. Lee to be photographed outside his home in Richmond, to which he had returned after his surrender at Appomattox. (see below)

Brady's artistic success with war did not lead to economic success with peace. After the war his business declined rapidly, and he went bankrupt in 1872. He had hoped to make a significant profit by selling his wartime photos to the federal government. He eventually did so, but at a much lower price than he had hoped. (This book contains copies of many of those photos, Brady's eternal legacy, which are on the web-site and/or in the files of the Library of Congress, loc.gov.)

Further Reading: Mary Panzer, *Mathew Brady and the Image of History* (Washington D.C.: Smithsonian, 1997; Theodore P. Savas, *Brady's Civil War Journal: Photographing the War, 1861-65*. New York: Skyhorse, 2008.

Braxton Bragg, His Own Worst Enemy?

Braxton Bragg and His Subordinates

Ulysses Grant wrote the following story about Confederate General Braxton Bragg in his memoirs. It seems that while serving on the frontier, he once held two different positions at a fort at the same time. Having made a mistake while serving in one, he brought charges against himself while serving in the other! Bragg referred the matter to his commanding officer, who responded, "My God, Mr. Bragg. You have quarreled with every officer in the army, and now you are quarrelling with yourself!" The story was likely apocryphal, but Grant's point was to underline the stiff, formal, uncompromising, cantankerous nature of the man.

Bragg and trouble were almost always close companions during the war, especially because he frequently acted in unexpected ways, almost always to his own detriment. Even when he won victories, he was disinclined to follow up because he lacked confidence in himself or in his subordinates, with whom he constantly quarreled and/or blamed for mistakes.

After his greatest victory, at Chickamauga, September 19-20, 1863, Bragg, commanding the Army of Tennessee, was beset by a rebellion of his subordinate generals. They believed, probably rightly, that the Union army was ready to be swept from the field and that Chattanooga was theirs for the taking. But Bragg did not act, rather spending several weeks reorganizing his army, even as the dismay of the subordinates increased.

Then, President Jefferson Davis, Bragg's close friend, visited the army to assess the situation. Despite the unanimous view of the subordinates, Davis kept Bragg as commander. The Union victories soon afterward at Lookout Mountain and Missionary Ridge and Bragg's precipitous retreat finally led Davis to replace him.

During his next assignment, as Davis's military advisor, Bragg did not command any troops. As a result, he performed well and provided useful input. However, in keeping with his character, he also undermined other commanders he did not like. Joseph Johnston's removal from command during the Atlanta campaign was influenced by Bragg's animosity.

After eight months in Richmond, Bragg returned to active duty in 1865. His objective was to protect the last remaining open Confederate port, Wilmington, as well as Fort Fisher, which protected access to Wilmington. Although the Confederates' situation there, as elsewhere, was desperate, and success was unlikely, Bragg's poor performance guaranteed the outcome. Then, as usual, he blamed others for his losses. In March 1865 he fought against Jacob Cox at the Battle of Wyse Forks, North Carolina. But after an advance the first day, once again he had to retreat. Bragg was with Davis when the latter fled Richmond, and he was later captured, then paroled.

Eminent historian James McPherson has posited that "bumblers like Bragg and Pemberton and Hood lost the West." But of course the Union forces led by Grant, Sherman, Thomas, and Schofield had a lot to do with it too. Today the U.S. army's Fort Bragg, like Fort Hood and others named after Confederate generals, are monuments to these men for reasons which many cannot comprehend. It appears likely that as part of the controversy over Confederate monuments, these "namings" may soon be due for filing into the dustbin of history.

(Below is a contemporary drawing of the Battle of Missionary Ridge)

Further Reading: Earl Hess, *Braxton Bragg: The Most Hated Man of the Confederacy.* Chapel Hill: University of North Carolina Press, 2016; Thomas Lawrence Connelly, *Army of the Heartland: The Army of Tennessee,* Baton Rouge: Louisiana State University Press, 1967.

John C. Breckinridge, Union and Confederate Statesman

John Breckinridge and Divided Loyalties

Kentucky was the birthplace of both Abraham Lincoln and Jefferson Davis, so it perhaps wasn't surprising that denizens of the state had divided loyalties during the Civil War era. While Kentucky declared itself neutral at first, both the Union and the Confederacy sought the loyalty of its people. John Breckinridge, one of the most esteemed, yet virtually forgotten politicians of this era, would be, like his divided state, loyal to both the Union and the Confederacy.

Born in Lexington of a prominent family, Breckinridge was a lawyer who served in the Mexican War, though he did not see any combat. After the war he was elected to Congress as a Democrat. His innate talents and the patronage of Henry Clay, Stephen Douglas, and Franklin Pierce made him a "coming man" in national politics. In 1856 he was the youngest man ever to be elected Vice-President, under Buchanan.

From 1859 to 1861 Breckinridge's career underwent mind-boggling changes, and in a sense he was a trailblazer because of these unique experiences. In 1859 as the secession crisis was accelerating, he was elected to the Senate from Kentucky, his term to begin in 1861 after he left the Vice Presidency. In 1860 he ran for president and received the second-most electoral votes, after Lincoln. In 1861 he supported Lincoln at first in the Senate, though he made sympathetic comments about the Confederacy and opposed military action to suppress the rebellion. In the fall he declared his support for the Confederacy, and on November 2, 1861, he was commissioned as a Confederate Brigadier General.

Breckinridge's military career included service in both the West and East, though he rarely commanded large elements of the rebel armies. He was in reserve at Shiloh, and during the Battle of Stones River he performed well. But, as in the case of so many other Confederate generals, afterwards he got into a dispute with commanding General Braxton Bragg, who Breckinridge thought was unworthy of command. Later, after Confederate defeats at Lookout Mountain and Missionary Ridge in 1863, Bragg blamed Breckinridge, alleging that he had been drunk. Subsequently Breckinridge helped win the Battles of New Market and Monocacy, joining Jubal Early on his raid into the outskirts of Washington.

In February 1865 Davis named Breckinridge Secretary of War. Recognizing that victory was unlikely, Breckinridge then began another series of mind-boggling events. When Richmond was abandoned in April and Davis fled, Breckenridge oversaw the destruction of supplies but also the preservation of Confederate records. He then traveled to join Lee, but after the latter surrendered, Breckenridge journeyed on to Greensboro to consult with Joe Johnston. After working with Sherman and Johnston on their surrender agreement, Breckinridge assisted Davis's ongoing efforts to evade pursuing Union troops. After Davis was captured, Breckinridge, fearing his own arrest, made his way to England. He returned to Kentucky in 1869, still then only 48 years old. He died in 1875.

(Below is an image of a poster for the 1860 election. Breckinridge is closest to Lincoln, as he would be in the election: The poster is of special interest because it uses baseball terminology and images, underlining that that sport had already become the "national game.")

Further Reading: William C. Davis, *Breckinridge: Statesman, Soldier, Symbol.* Baton Rouge: Louisiana State University Press, 1974; James C. Klotter, *Breckinridges of Kentucky, 1760-1981.* University Press of Kentucky, 1986.

Ben "Beast" Butler

Ben Butler, the Most Hated Man in New Orleans History

Ben Butler's military record is, to say the least, checkered. But in almost every position he held, he was either a troublemaker or a trailblazer, and sometimes both! This oft-criticized "Political General" was a Massachusetts lawyer and politician before the war. As a leading war Democrat, Butler's ambitions for a military office were encouraged by Lincoln as a means of further uniting the parties to support the war effort. Butler was given a Brigadier Generalship in the U.S. Volunteers, and he later rose to the rank of Major General.

Early in the war, he led Massachusetts militia to put down a riot in Baltimore, a key step in holding that state for the Union. Later, while stationed in Virginia, he devised the concept of "contraband of war" in refusing to return escaped slaves to their "owners." That innovation soon became Union policy, and it helped pave the way for the Emancipation Proclamation. In mid-1862 he led the land forces which took the city of New Orleans, effectively sealing Union control of the southern part of the Mississippi River. While military commander of New Orleans, Butler innovated public health measures which saved countless lives in that swampy, humid climate.

Butler has not received sufficient credit for the above-noted trailblazing elements of his career, in part because of his problems and troublemaking in other endeavors. During his tenure in New Orleans, Butler placed firm controls on the angry population, which resisted in a variety of ways. Many women would, for example, turn their backs on the street when soldiers walked by and would make critical comments about the Union. In response, Butler instituted a policy that any woman who did not respect U.S. soldiers would be considered as a prostitute subject to arrest. That step was the proximate cause of the creation of the "Butler Chamber Pot, "which is still sold in New Orleans, where Ben Butler continues to be the most hated man in its history.

Later in the war Butler mismanaged several military commands, and he was finally removed from active military duty in late 1864. However, he returned to Congress and was one of the most avid prosecutors of the impeached Andrew Johnson. Later, he was one of the strongest defenders of Grant during his presidency, dismissing any and all charges of corruption in that administration.

In sum, Ben Butler was one of the most colorful characters of the Civil War era, a man whose several positive contributions are overshadowed by his many foibles and failures.

(Below is an image of the "Butler Chamber Pot" placed appropriately in a 19th century toilet seat. The device is today in a prominent place in a Vicksburg mansion)

Further Reading: Ben Butler, *Autobiography and Personal Reminiscences of Major-General Benj. F. Butler.* A. M. Thayer, 1892 (otherwise known as "Butler's Book"); Richard Wedgewick West, *Lincoln's Scapegoat General: A Life of Benjamin F. Butler, 1818–1893.* Boston: Houghton Mifflin, 1965; . Hans L. Trefousse, *Ben Butler: The South Called Him Beast!.* New York: Twayne, 1957.

33

Patrick Cleburne, Trailblazer and Troublemaker Both

Patrick Cleburne and the Price of Integrity

Perhaps frustrated with both the leadership of his commander, John Bell Hood, and his treatment at the hands of the Confederate leadership, Patrick Cleburne made a memorable statement at the Battle of Franklin, November 30, 1864: "If we are to die, let us die like men." Leading from the front, he charged toward the Union line and encouraged his men forward. He was shot and killed, as were over 1700 soldiers that bloody day.

Cleburne was born in Ireland and had served in the British army before emigrating to the United States. He eventually settled in Helena, Arkansas, where he became a lawyer and a leading citizen. When the war broke out, he sided with the Confederacy, and because of his military background was soon made a general. He fought successfully at the Battles of Shiloh, Perryville, Stones River, Chickamauga, and Missionary Ridge, creating a reputation as a hard fighter and highly-respected leader. Some began to call him "Stonewall of the West," but unlike his namesake he did not get promoted to senior levels, perhaps because of his foreign birth.

In early 1864 Cleburne, with a perspective which native-born Southerners did not have, realized that the Confederate cause was in peril in the long term. He adjudged that the Union's deployment of black troops in large numbers would only accelerate the Confederacy's difficulties. In response he had a visionary idea. Hoping that his prestige might carry the day, he held a meeting of subordinate generals of the Army of Tennessee and proposed that the Confederacy too consider arming black troops. As part of his idea, he suggested that the Confederate government "guarantee freedom within a reasonable time to every slave in the South who shall remain true to the Confederacy."

Cleburne's proposal gained almost no support among the other generals, and it was ultimately used by some to block his further promotion. Further, when it was sent on to Richmond for consideration by the government, Jefferson Davis ordered that the proposal be expunged from the record of the war. The evidence of this trailblazing idea was not found until the release of the Official Records.

The irony is that in March 1865, when the Confederacy was in even more desperate straits, Davis proposed a similar measure to the Confederate Congress. It passed, but it was never implemented.

As for Cleburne, he did "die like a man" that day at Franklin leading his troops in the final massive frontal infantry attack of the war. By then his vision had been quashed, but ultimately it would not be forgotten. It remains today a significant part of his legacy.

(Below is the Kurz and Allison painting of the Battle of Franklin)

_____Further Reading: Craig Symonds, *Stonewall of the West: Patrick Cleburne and the Civil War*. Lawrence: University Press of Kansas, 1997; Bruce H. Stewart, *Invisible Hero: Patrick R. Cleburne*. Macon, GA: Mercer University Press, 2009.

BATTLE OF FRANKLIN.

Jacob Cox, Citizen General

Jacob Cox and a Citizens' Army

"The army must be a unit, because if the regular army organization is so narrow it can't be expanded in time of emergency, what use is it? If a volunteer organization is fit to decide the *great* wars of the nation, is it not ridiculous to keep an expensive organization of regulars for the petty contests with Indians or for an ornamental appendage to the State in peace? The thing to be aimed at is to have a system flexible enough to provide for the increase of the army to any size required, without losing any of the advantage of character or efficiency which, in any respect, pertained to it as a regular army."

General Jacob Cox wrote those sentiments to his friend Secretary of the Treasury Salmon P. Chase on January 1, 1863. They reflected both his frustration with how he, a "citizen general" with no formal training, and others in that category were being treated, and his thoughts about how the army should be reformed.

When the war began, General-in-Chief Winfield Scott had created the "United States Volunteers" as what he foresaw as an auxiliary to the regular army. Reflecting his negative experiences with volunteer soldiers, Scott envisioned regular soldiers doing the bulk of the fighting and volunteers only guarding the borders and the rivers. His expectations for a short war apparently convinced him that the then 16,000 man army was sufficient, even though nearly a third of that number defected to the Confederacy.

Ultimately Scott's vision proved wrong, and over 2 million men joined the Union forces. But because of his decision, most of those men were not in the army – they were in the "U.S. Volunteers." This was true of men at all ranks, up to and including two-star generals (the highest rank at the time). Inevitably, West Point-trained professional soldiers looked down on self-made soldiers. This rivalry was a major hindrance on the Union army, especially as all senior commands went to West Pointers. General-in-chief Henry Halleck once said that to give commands to "Political Generals" was simply murder, and that view affected command assignments. .

Jacob Cox, a Citizen-General from Ohio who served capably throughout the war, saw the effect of this division several times in his military career. For example, Henry Benham, a West Pointer, failed miserably during the West Virginia campaign, while Cox won praise from his commanders George McClellan and William Rosecrans. Cox could only be appalled later when Benham, who was arrested for misconduct twice during the War, still was returned to duty. In his *Military Reminiscences*, Cox delved extensively into the theme that the U.S. should follow Napoleon's example of creating a "citizens army." He emphasized that it was not in a schoolroom, but only on the battlefield that one could determine "military aptitude."

Over time the U.S. military has slowly evolved into the kind of organization Cox envisioned. The fact that General George Marshall, a firm advocate of a citizens army, could attain a 5-star rank without a West Point education underscored the transition. Colin Powell's ROTC training was not a hindrance to his becoming Chairman of the Joint Chiefs of Staff. Today the leadership of the U.S. military has a broad range of backgrounds, and formal training in one of the academies is not a requirement. While Jacob Cox was not alone in his vision of how to create a modern army, his extensive thinking about it, made in the middle of the Civil War, illustrate both his foresight and the accuracy of his thinking. The biography of Cox discusses these concepts. (see below)

Further Reading: Eugene Schmiel, *Citizen-General: Jacob Dolson Cox and the Civil War Era*, (Athens: Ohio University Press, 2014); and Thomas J. Goss, *The War Within the Union High Command: Politics and Generalship During the Civil War*, (Lawrence: The University of Kansas Press, 2003).

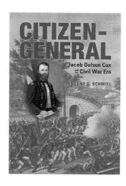

Chapter II: *Lost Causers, Heroes, and a Crusader*

This group includes people who caused major problems by acting in what they thought was the national interest, and others who overcame great difficulties to help resolve some of those problems.

Union General **Jefferson C. Davis**, (1828-1879) despite his name, was a staunch Unionist who made major errors in judgment.

Frederick Douglass (1817-1895) was the most famous and influential freedman of the era.

Confederate General **Jubal Early** (1816-1894) was a mediocre fighter who was primarily responsible for creating the myth the "Lost Cause."

Sarah Emma Edmonds (1841-1898), AKA Private Frank Thompson, was a Union spy who fought under her male pseudonym.

John Floyd, (1808-1863) former Virginia governor and Secretary of War under President Buchanan, undercut the Union by shifting resources to the South in the days before Fort Sumter.

Confederate General **Nathan Bedford Forrest** (1821-1877) was a superb fighter and cavalryman whose prewar career as a slaver and postwar support of the Ku Klux Klan have tarnished his reputation.

Union General **William Franklin** (1823-1903) caused significant problems for his superior officers because of his timidity and perfidy.

John C. Fremont, (1813-1890) Republican Presidential Candidate in 1856 and an esteemed explorer, proved incompetent as a general.

Richard Gatling (1818-1903) is famous for his namesake gun, which, like many other inventions, made war more efficient and bloody.

Rose O'Neal Greenhow (1813-1864) was one of the best Confederate spies during the war.

Jefferson Davis of the Union

Jefferson C. Davis's Misjudgments

This Jefferson Davis was unique not only because he had the same name as the Confederate President. First, he enlisted in the army during the Mexican War and remained in it his entire life. Second, he murdered his commanding officer in 1862, but was not convicted. Third, on Sherman's "March to the Sea," he deliberately dismantled a pontoon bridge which left following slaves to drown or be recaptured. But his biographers, after acknowledging these realities, aver that, "the smoke of notoriety, however, obscures the military leader, a general officer admired by Sherman and repeatedly given increased responsibility." In other words, he was a troublemaker, but should not be judged solely on the basis of his awful misjudgments.

When the war began, Davis had risen to the rank of lieutenant, but the exigencies of the war and his experience led to his promotion to Brigadier General of Volunteers in 1862. He performed well under Grant and John C. Fremont in the West, but in late September, 1862, he and his commander, General William "Bull" Nelson, quarreled over perceived personal slights. Davis shot and killed Nelson in public, and he presumed he would be court-martialed. However, because of the need for skilled leaders, he was not tried. He never received another promotion, which presumably was his only punishment.

Davis served ably at Stones River and Chickamauga, and during the Atlanta campaign he became commander of the XIVth corps. He retained that position for the rest of the war. On the March to the Sea, on December 9, 1864, Davis apparently deliberately ordered a pontoon bridge removed before hundreds of former slaves, who were following his corps, could cross the creek. Many were captured by following Confederates cavalry or drowned in the creek while they attempted to escape.

There was allegedly only one incident during the war when the fact that Davis shared his name with the Confederate president caused a problem. During the Battle of Chickamauga in 1863, as dusk descended, soldiers of the 21st Ohio noticed a bevy of men approaching their position. Their first instinct was to hope they were Union reinforcements, but they remained suspicious. As the unidentified troops moved closer like wraiths in the twilight, one Union soldier called out, "What troops are you?" The collective response was "Jeff Davis's troops." The Ohio soldiers let out a sigh of relief, confident that the oncoming men referred to their Union general. A short while later, they were staring at the drawn muzzles of the 7th Florida. The Ohioans promptly surrendered.

While this Jefferson Davis's contributions to the Union effort were manifold and mainly positive, his legacy will always be overshadowed by his troublemaking actions which showed an almost-incredible lack of judgment.

(Below is an image of Davis leading his XIVth corps during the Grand Review of the Armies in Washington, May 24, 1865).

Further Reading: Nathaniel Hughes and Gordon Whitney, *Jefferson Davis in Blue: The Life of Sherman's Relentless Warrior.* Baton Rouge: LSU Press, 2002; Noah Andrew Trudeau, *Southern Storm: Sherman's March to the Sea.* New York: HarperCollins, 2008

Frederick Douglass, Crusader

Frederick Douglass

He was the nation's conscience, reminding 19th century American society at every possible turn of its wrongs and recommending how to make them right. He was a trailblazer in racial politics upon whose legacy all future activists would operate. His relationship with Abraham Lincoln would play an important positive role in the evolution of race relations in the United States.

Born into slavery, Douglass escaped from Maryland to New York in 1839 when he was twenty-one. He soon became involved in abolitionism, giving public speeches and writing for newspapers. His autobiography, *Narrative of the Life of Frederick Douglass,* sold well, and he became both a celebrity and the object of attacks by anti-abolitionists in the North.

During the 1850s Douglass saw the rise of the Republican Party as a mixed blessing. While pleased that it opposed the expansion of slavery, he regretted that it did not support black rights. While he did not advocate for Lincoln's election in 1860, he saw Lincoln as preferable to the alternatives. This suspicion of Lincoln and his motives would eventually change into admiration and support as Lincoln's policies evolved, in part due to Douglass's incessant and fervent lobbying.

Douglass was pleasantly surprised when Lincoln called for volunteers after the attack on Fort Sumter, and he praised the war as the means, potentially, of destroying slavery. Though for political reasons Lincoln did not advocate the end of slavery for a time, Douglass actively promulgated the idea that slavery was the cause of the war and that the war's objective should be abolition. He agitated for allowing blacks to join the army, and this advocacy was one of the keys to that provision being included in the Emancipation Proclamation.

Douglass met with Lincoln three times (see above) during the Civil War, which allowed him to use his significant persuasive skills to push and nudge Lincoln into preferred directions. While Douglass believed that Lincoln was slowly evolving into a believer in equality, he continued to advocate for improvements, such as equal pay for black troops. Douglass was also one of the most active recruiters of black troops, arguing publicly that their service justified their being given equal rights after the war.

Lincoln's assassination ended this important partnership for the advancement of black rights.

In 1876 at the dedication ceremonies of the Emancipation Proclamation monument in Washington, Douglass said, "Can any colored man, or any white man friendly to the freedom of all men, ever forget the night which followed the first day of January 1863, when the world was to see if Abraham Lincoln would prove to be as good as his word?...Though Mr. Lincoln shared the prejudices of his white fellow-countrymen against the Negro, it is hardly necessary to say that in his heart of hearts he loathed and hated slavery."

Further Reading: William S. McFeely, *Frederick Douglass*. New York: W.W. Norton, 1991; James Oakes, *The Radical and the Republican: Frederick Douglass, Abraham Lincoln, and the Triumph of Antislavery Politics*. New York: W.W. Norton, 2007.

THE LATE GENERAL JUBAL A. EARLY.

Jubal Early, Founder of the Myth of the Lost Cause

Robert E. Lee called Early his "bad old man," though it isn't clear whether the sobriquet was affectionate or even accurate. Early had an adequate military career as a subordinate of both Stonewall Jackson and Richard Ewell in Lee's Army of Northern Virginia. He is perhaps most famous for his raid on Washington late in the war which, for a time, threatened the city, and during which Lincoln, observing the fighting, came under fire.

Early is infamous for his raid into Pennsylvania in the days before the Battle of Gettysburg. He skirmished with state militia on June 26, 1863, then seized the town of Chambersburg, population 2,000. He demanded a ransom before leaving town, which was paid. On June 28, Early held York, the largest town to fall in the North during the entire war, for $100,000 in ransom. Later, as part of his mythologizing of the Confederacy, Early emphasized the gallant treatment meted out to all civilians by all Confederate troops, as compared to the vicious treatment meted out by Union troops. He clearly had no sense of irony.

After the war, in part to deflect from his own failures at the critical Battle of Gettysburg, Early trailblazed the movement known as the "Lost Cause." That belief system deified Lee, claimed the antebellum Southern way of life was superior to the North's, and asserted that the Confederacy lost solely because of overwhelming Union numbers. In speeches throughout the South and in articles in Confederate Veterans' magazines, Early pushed these theses and successfully encouraged others to do so. As part of that process, Early fingered General James Longstreet as the *bete noire* of the defeat at Gettysburg. He claimed that Longstreet failed to carry out Lee's orders, and that if he had done so, Gettysburg would have been a key to Confederate victory.

The Lost Cause myth was the foundation of teaching about the war for many years in both North and South. It remains today a powerful reminder that myths often retain a stronger hold on popular memory than facts. The construction of hundreds of statues and memorials to the Confederacy during the 19th and 20th centuries, and the controversy over their status are among the after-effects of Early's role in the creation of a powerful myth.

Further Reading: Gary Gallagher & Alan T. Nolan, eds. *The Myth of the Lost Cause and Civil War History.* Bloomington: Indiana University Press, 2000; Blight, David W. *Race and Reunion: The Civil War in American Memory.* Cambridge, MA & London: Belknap Press of Harvard University Press, 2001; Benjamin F. Cooling, *Robert E. Lee's Bad Old Man.* New York: Rowman and Littlefield, 2014).

(Below is an image of a "Lost Cause" banner of the era)

Sarah Emma Edmonds, AKA Private Franklin Thompson

Nurse and Spy in the Union Army
The Adventures and Experiences of a Woman ...

S. EMMA E. EDMONDS

A PUBLIC DOMAIN BOOK

Sarah Emma Edmonds, Person of Many Identities

Most women, other than nurses, played their roles during the Civil War behind the scenes, not on the battlefield. The sensibilities of the era "protected" them from being exposed to the brutalities of war. But those same customs on occasion allowed them to play "male" roles through subterfuge, especially since there was no physical examination to become a soldier. Sarah Edmonds was one of hundreds of women who fought as men in the Civil War.

Born in Canada, she escaped a difficult family situation by moving to Flint, Michigan in 1856 at the age of 15. To make a living she became a book salesman disguised as a man named "Franklin Thompson." When the war began, she enlisted as a male nurse under that pseudonym. Private Thompson participated in a variety of roles, including courier and mailman, in the Peninsula campaign, and at the Battles of Second Manassas, Antietam, and Fredericksburg. Several times she was called upon to actually fire a weapon, and she performed adequately. She also claimed to have acted as a spy for the Union, allegedly assuming three separate identities to gain critical information for her military superiors. However, there is no official record of her service in that capacity. (Her autobiography is the primary source for the claims of her actions as a Union spy).

At some point in 1864, she contracted malaria. Realizing that she could not be treated medically lest her female identity be discovered, Franklin Thompson "deserted" and Sarah Edmonds became a nurse at a military hospital in Washington. In 1865 she published a best-selling autobiography, *Nurse and Spy in the Union Army* and became a celebrity. Eventually, "Thompson" received an honorable discharge and a military pension. She later became the first and only female member of the most important Union veterans group, the Grand Army of the Republic (GAR). In 1901 she was buried in the GAR's Houston cemetery following a full military funeral.

(Below is a placard of the "GAR and Its Supporters." Note Clara Barton, "Mother" Bickerdyke, and other women are pictured, but it does not appear that Sarah Edmonds is there).

Further Reading: Sylvia G. Dannett, *She Rode with the Generals: the True and Incredible Story of Sarah Emma Seelye, alias Franklin Thompson*. Thomas Nelson and Sons, 1960; . Karen Abbott, *Liar, Temptress, Soldier, Spy: Four Women Undercover in the Civil War.* HarperCollins, 2014

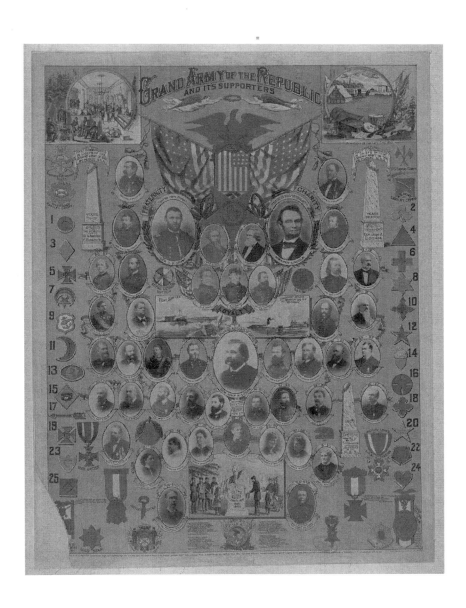

John Floyd, Military Failure

John B. Floyd, Confederate Zealot

President James Buchanan's biographer aptly summarized the failures of that administration thusly:

"Buchanan's failing during the crisis over the Union was not inactivity but rather his partiality for the South, a favoritism that bordered on disloyalty...By any measure Buchanan appeased the South; he allowed his cabinet officers to send weapons to the South; he allowed southerners to gain time and confidence so that when the war started the North faced a powerful enemy."

Buchanan's Secretary of War, John B. Floyd, a former governor of Virginia, had been engaged in a variety of corrupt schemes during his Cabinet tenure. But Buchanan let him resign in December 1860 before charges could be brought. Earlier, as Grant wrote in his memoirs, "Floyd scattered the army so that much of it could be captured when hostilities should commence, and distributed the cannon and small arms from Northern arsenals throughout the South so as to be on hand when treason wanted them. The navy was scattered in like manner." Every decision was legal, but each was harmful to the cause of the Union. Floyd was ultimately indicted for corruption, but he was never brought to trial.

When the war began, Floyd took up arms as a Confederate general, but failed miserably. In western Virginia he feuded with another military commander and former Virginia governor, Henry Wise. At one point their united forces could have overwhelmed William Rosecrans's Union army. Instead, they refused to cooperate, despite the urging of General Robert E. Lee. Ultimately, Wise was removed, but the now-united forces under Floyd were nevertheless defeated in November 1861, forcing his precipitous retreat. This Confederate defeat was a major step opening the way for creation of the state of West Virginia.

Floyd's political status and prestige got him a new command in early 1862 at Fort Donelson in Tennessee. He performed as well there as he had in West Virginia. Soon after taking command, Floyd was threatened by an advance by Ulysses Grant, whose campaign against this facility and Fort Henry were critically-important steps leading to Union control in the West.

Grant's superior forces quickly put Fort Donelson in danger, and Floyd and his subordinates agreed on February 14 to surrender. But Floyd abandoned his post, fearing he would be arrested. His deputy commander, General Gideon Pillow, also deserted, leaving General Simon Bolivar Buckner to accept Grant's terms of "unconditional surrender," a critical step in establishing his reputation as a great commander. Floyd died in 1863, his legacy as a troublemaker and incompetent in both civilian and military policy firmly established.

(Below is an image of the Buchanan cabinet, with Floyd to Buchanan's right).

Further Reading: Jean H. Baker, *James Buchanan.* New York: Times Books, 2004; also see Ezra J. Warner, *Generals in Gray: Lives of the Confederate Commanders.* Baton Rouge: Louisiana State University Press, 1959; and Michael Birkner, *James Buchanan and the Coming of the Civil War.* Gainesville: University of Florida Press, 2013.

Nathan Bedford Forrest, Cavalryman par Excellence

Nathan Bedford Forrest: Slavery and the Klan

Few Confederate commanders struck more fear into the heart of Union commanders than Nathan Bedford Forrest. Perhaps the best Confederate "Political General," his ruthless and dynamic approach to fighting and the deployment of his cavalry brought him a legacy of multiple military successes.

Forrest enlisted as a private, even though before the war he had been a successful businessman, including as an active slave trader. Early in the war he exhibited his cavalry and leadership skills by successfully covering retreats from Fort Donelson and Shiloh. He became a Brigadier General in July 1862 and began the extensive raiding of Union supplies and forces for which he would become famous. At one point he destroyed Grant's supply line during the Vicksburg campaign. Forrest played a critical role at Chickamauga, harassing the retreating Union soldiers to help solidify the Confederate victory. However, like many others, he soon got into a dispute with army commander Braxton Bragg because the latter did not follow up this victory.

In April 1864 Forrest engaged in his most controversial battle. After his men had taken the Union's Fort Pillow, they massacred many of the surrendered Union soldiers, including a significant number of U.S. Colored Troops. Most historians agree there was a bloodbath, but disagree on Forrest's specific role. On the other hand, it was the men under his command who committed the atrocities.

Late in 1864 Forrest played an important role in the Franklin-Nashville campaign supporting John Bell Hood. However, he failed in his key mission to cut off the Union force under John Schofield at Spring Hill, Tennessee. Before the Battle of Franklin, November 30, 1864, Forrest, along with many other subordinates, argued against the frontal attack Hood ordered. Later, after Hood's army was almost destroyed at the Battle of Nashville, Forrest skillfully screened its retreat. In his last military action, Forrest failed to fend off James Wilson's cavalry campaign into Mississippi, and he surrendered on May 9, 1865.

After the war Forrest engaged in several business ventures, but was never prosperous again. At some time in 1866 or 1867 he became involved in the Ku Klux Klan, and some sources say that he became its "Grand Wizard." Forrest testified before Congress in 1871 and denied that he was a member of the group. Subsequently he made speeches and made public gestures indicating that he supported black advancement. In sum, Forrest remained controversial.

As of the early 21st century, there were over 30 historical markers dedicated to Forrest in Tennessee, further underlining the controversy over the man's legacy. One of them, a statue in Memphis, was removed in 2017 after public protests, a trend which continues to gain momentum.

(Below is an image of that (former) statue of Forrest in Memphis).

Further Reading: Brian Steel Wills, *A Battle From the Start: The Life of Nathan Bedford Forrest.* New York: Harper Collins, 1992; Elaine Frantze Parsons, *Ku-Klux: The Birth of the Klan during Reconstruction.* Chapel Hill: University of North Carolina Press, 2016.

William Franklin, Undependable Soldier

Franklin's Fredericksburg Failures

The names Franklin, McClellan, and Porter will always be firmly linked in Civil War history. Franklin and Fitz-John Porter were what Lincoln called "McClellan's pets," the only senior officers with whom General George McClellan seemingly ever consulted during his campaigns. The fact that both men were sycophants underlines both McClellan's weakness and his narcissism.

Franklin graduated first in his 1843 class at West Point. As usual in that era, he entered the topographical engineer corps. He served in the Mexican War, and in 1859 took over the job of supervising construction of the U.S. Capitol from General Montgomery Meigs, the greatest unsung hero of the Civil War.

Franklin fought at First Bull Run, then became a Brigadier General of Volunteers in the Army of the Potomac, under his close friend McClellan. He led the VIth corps in the Peninsular Campaign, but saw little action. He was ordered to join Pope's Army of Virginia outside Washington, but he arrived too late to be of much assistance, in great part because of McClellan's slow response to the order. Pope later brought charges against Franklin, but they were dismissed.

During the Maryland campaign, Franklin commanded one wing of McClellan's army. He successfully pushed back a Confederate force at Crampton's Gap during the Battle of South Mountain. But the success came only because his subordinates, ignoring Franklin's overly-cautious approach, launched an attack . At the Battle of Antietam Franklin was in reserve when, according to an article he wrote in *Battles and Leaders of the Civil War,* he saw an opportunity at a critical moment to destroy the rebel center. He was right, but McClellan did not accept his recommendation.

When McClellan was replaced by Burnside, Franklin, ever the McClellan acolyte, suspected that Burnside had gotten the job by undercutting Little Mac. Despite this animosity, Burnside appointed Franklin as commander of his left wing. During the subsequent Battle of Fredericksburg (see below), Franklin performed poorly. Burnside's chances for success depended on a forceful attack by Franklin's left wing, but aggressiveness was something he usually lacked. It was a major Union defeat.

Franklin became more aggressive after the disastrous defeat, but in a very different way. He wrote to Lincoln complaining about Burnside's leadership and sent two subordinate generals to Washington to do so directly. In the ensuing contretemps, both Burnside and Franklin were removed. Franklin later served in the West, including in the Red River campaign, but he was wounded and was not given any additional assignments.

Broadly speaking, Franklin's contributions to the Union victory were minimal, in great part due to his timidity and his excessive loyalty to McClellan. His contempt for the chain of command and his insubordination towards Burnside were contemptible troublemaking.

(Below is an image of the Battle of Fredericksburg)

Further Reading: Mark A. Snell, *From First to Last: The Life of Major General William B. Franklin,* New York: Fordham University Press, 2002; William Marvel, *Burnside.* Chapel Hill: University of North Carolina Press, 1991.

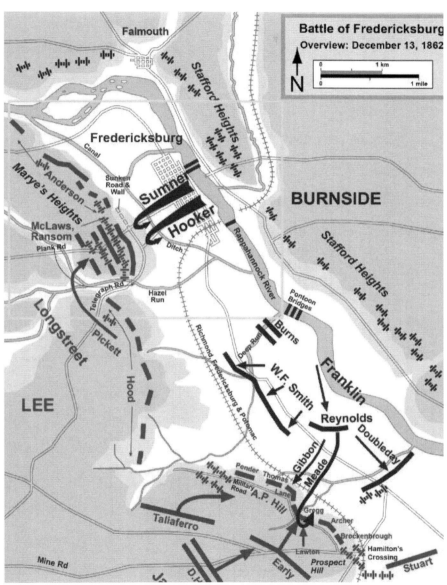

John C. Fremont, The Pathfinder

Fremont, Military Mediocrity

Until "The Pathfinder" crashed against "The Stonewall" in the 1862 Shenandoah campaign, John C. Fremont was considered one of the greatest Americans of the 19th century. His published accounts of his legendary trailblazing explorations in the West in the 1840's and 1850's earned him that nickname and encouraged westward expansion and settlement. He was the first Republican candidate for President, in 1856.

Those credentials and his service in the Mexican War earned him command of "The Department of the West" when the Civil War began. However, he proved to be a poor administrator and military leader, as well as a controversial politician. His 1861 declaration freeing slaves in Missouri was reversed by Lincoln, fearing it might lose the loyalty of the border states, especially Kentucky.

Lincoln fired Fremont after this contretemps, but was forced by anti-slavery Republicans to give Fremont another position. In early 1862 Lincoln created the Mountain Department under Fremont. His first objective was to take control of the Shenandoah Valley of Virginia and then move south to liberate eastern Tennessee. Unfortunately for Fremont, the ensuing campaign would prove to be a crowning achievement in the career of Confederate General Thomas "Stonewall" Jackson.

A Virginian who could rely on the support and information of the residents of the Valley as well as the maps of Jed Hotchkiss, Jackson defeated Fremont and his allied forces during May and June, 1862. His twists and turns up and down the valley confused the Union commanders and allowed him to defeat an overall force double his size. Fremont, who had expected the campaign to lead to greater military glories (see the stylized image below), was fired once again, and he would not get another assignment. Fremont's postwar career consisted of a slow slide into obscurity, although some anti-slavery Republicans wanted to nominate him for president in 1864.

Fremont's career was mixed: great successes and great failures. He was a great trailblazer as an explorer, but also a significant troublemaker in the political and military spheres.

(Below is a stylized image of Fremont leading his forces)

Further Reading: Jacob Cox, "Fremont in West Virginia," *Battles and Leaders of the Civil War*. New York: 1882—8; Peter Cozzens, *Shenandoah 1862: Stonewall Jackson's 1862 Valley Campaign*. Chapel Hill: University of North Carolina Press, 2008.

Richard Gatling, Inventor

Richard Gatling and the Efficiency of Modern War

Looking back on his creation, the Gatling Gun, Richard Gatling wrote in 1877, "It occurred to me that if I could invent a machine – a gun – which could by its rapidity of fire, enable one man to do as much battle duty as a hundred, that it would, to a large extent supersede the necessity of large armies, and consequently, exposure to battle and disease [would] be greatly diminished."

In 1888 Albert Nobel, the inventor of dynamite, was disturbed by an erroneous report of his death which was headlined, "The Merchant of Death is Dead." One of his reactions was to create the Nobel Prizes. Gatling, as far as we know, did not similarly recognize the irony of his vision of his destructive creation.

Gatling was celebrated in the nineteenth century as a trailblazing and innovative genius. His inventions included a machine for sowing seeds and a steam plow, both of which were critical to the growth and strength of American agriculture. The Gatling Gun, his legacy and namesake, was based on the sowing machine, and he patented it in 1861.

In part because of resistance to change and untraditional methodology by the ordnance department of the Union army, only a few of these guns were bought and used by the Union army during the Civil War. The same was true of other significant innovations such as the repeater rifle.

Would the war have been much shorter if Union soldiers had had repeaters and the Gatling gun as early as 1863 in large numbers? We can only speculate -- but it certainly would not have been longer! In an interesting, but sad side-note: at Custer's last stand, some of the Indians had repeater rifles, but none of Custer's men did.. Eventually, the Gatling Gun and similar weapons were accepted by armies around the world. However, Gatling's 1877 wishful thinking about the impact of such weapons clearly did not come about.

Further Reading: Julia Keller, *Mr. Gatling's Terrible Marvel: The Gun That Changed Everything and the Misunderstood Genius Who Invented It*, (New York: Viking, 2008); Jack Coggins, *Arms and Equipment of the Civil War.* Dover Publications, 2012..

(The image below is a satirical look at how an "intellectual gatling gun" is used by "Science against Superstition.")

Rose O'Neal Greenhow, Spy

Rose O'Neal Greenhow and Loyalty

Both trailblazer and troublemaker, Greenhow was a major figure in the Civil War despite her attempts to do her work as a spy *sub rosa*. Relying on the fact that most men would never suspect a woman of being capable of such subterfuge, she was able to provide significant intelligence to the Confederacy until her death in 1864.

Greenhow had lived in Washington for many years before beginning her work as a leading Confederate spymaster in 1861. She reportedly had been enamored of John C. Calhoun, the South Carolina Senator who was the most outspoken advocate of the importance of slavery and "Southern culture." Early in the war, Greenhow gained her information from a variety of sources, including from one of her lovers, Senator Henry Wilson, chairman of the Military Affairs Committee. That helped lead to her first success, sending Union Commander Irvin McDowell's plan for the First Battle of Bull Run to Confederate commander P.G. T. Beauregard.

Unfortunately for Rose, one man who did suspect her activities was Allan Pinkerton, the head of the newly-minted Union Secret Service. He and his men watched Greenhow's residence for weeks after that battle, looking for evidence. Pinkerton ultimately placed her under house arrest, and then put her in prison in Washington in early 1862. Her youngest daughter, Rose, age 8, was allowed to stay with her. (see picture below)

During her captivity Greenhow continued to work with her network of spies and pass messages and information to the Confederacy. She was freed in May 1862 on the understanding that she would be exiled to the South and not return until after the war. She was sent first to Fort Monroe, Virginia, and on her subsequent arrival in Richmond, was greeted as a hero.

.

Later, Jefferson Davis sent her as an emissary to England and France to assist in the effort to gain diplomatic recognition. While there she wrote her autobiography, *My Imprisonment and the First Year of Abolition Rule at Washington*. She tried to return to the U.S. in 1864 by boat. But when she tried to get away from a pursuing Union ship in a small boat, she was washed overboard and drowned, allegedly weighed down by gold coins from the earnings from her book. After her body was found, she was given a Confederate military funeral in Wilmington, North Carolina.

Further Reading: Karen Abbott, *Liar, Temptress, Soldier, Spy:Four Women Undercover in the Civil War*. HarperCollins, 2014; Ann Blackman, *Wild Rose: Rose O'Neal Greenhow, Confederate Spy*. Random House, 2005.

Chapter III: *Leaders, Incompetents, and Innovators*

The next group includes two presidents with different reputations and a variety of Civil War actors, some of whose intense focus on their own self-interest clouded their understanding of the national interest..

Union General **Henry Halleck** (1815-1872) was a mediocre military chief-of-staff whose bureaucratic approach to policy confused his subordinates and his leaders.

Confederate General **John Bell Hood** (1831-1879) was a superb corps commander whose commitment to outmoded tactics as an army commander led to the destruction of the Army of Tennessee.

Union General **Joe Hooker** (1814-1879) had all the elements of a superb military leader, but talked a better game than he played.

Union General **Alvin Hovey** (1821-1891) lobbied strenuously for promotion after abandoning the field of battle.

Union General **Henry Hunt** (1819-1889) was a superb artillery commander whose guns played a critical role at Gettysburg.

Andrew Johnson (1808-1875) may have been the worst U.S. President. His decisions contributed to 150 years of racial conflict.

Union General **Judson Kilpatrick**'s (1836-1881) reputation as a careless cavalry commander earned him the nickname "Kill Cavalry."

Union General **James H. Ledlie** (1832-1882) was drunk on duty, contributing significantly to the disastrous "Battle of the Crater."

Dr. Jonathan Letterman (1824-1872) contributed many innovations in medical care during his service to the Army of the Potomac.

Abraham Lincoln (1809-1865) was not only an effective President, but also one of the best "Political Generals" of the Union.

Henry Halleck, General-in-Chief

Henry Halleck and the Art of Obfuscation

He was called "Old Brains" because of his academic style, his command of the concepts of military warfare, and the books he wrote about tactics and strategy. However, when it came to fulfilling the practical elements of the position of General-In-Chief of the Union Army, Halleck was not up to the job. In many ways he fulfilled the stereotypical image of the academic, always thinking about options and possibilities, never able to make a decision or stand by it.

Halleck had performed adequately early in the war as commander of all western forces. However, he developed a reputation for moving excruciatingly slowly and carefully. Also, and underlining his lack of judgment, he had judged Grant to be an inadequate commander and had undercut him on several occasions, even after his victories. Halleck was called to Washington in 1862 to become General-in-Chief in part because of Lincoln's dissatisfaction with McClellan's Peninsula campaign. Lincoln told McClellan that the decision would allow him to concentrate on his duties near Richmond, but McClellan surmised that Lincoln and Stanton wanted to reduce his power and influence. For his part, Lincoln hoped that in Halleck he would have a military adviser whose expertise and decisiveness would be a key to mapping overall strategy and tactics. He was to be sorely disappointed.

Halleck's first major challenge was to ensure that, after McClellan was ordered to return from the Peninsula, sufficient forces were able to reinforce John Pope's Army of Virginia before Lee could attack. It did not happen. Halleck's messages to his commanders were written by a commanding general unsure of himself and of the location of his forces. After the defeat at Second Bull Run, Lincoln treated Halleck more as a glorified clerk than military commander.

During the Maryland campaign Halleck's dithering and almost-Delphic messages provided him with an "out" and excuse for failure no matter what McClellan did against Lee. Also, Halleck's decision to keep troops at Harpers Ferry led to the largest surrender of U. S. army forces in history. His hectoring of McClellan about ensuring that Lee did not attack Washington annoyed McClellan to distraction. Later, Halleck's inattention and tardy supply of pontoons to Burnside led to delays in the latter's advance toward Fredericksburg and, arguably, the subsequent defeat there.

When Grant became General-in-Chief in 1864, Halleck became Chief of Staff, an administrative position which suited his risk-averse and blame-deflecting personality. He performed his role under Grant's authority very effectively. But when Lincoln died, he and many in Washington became unnerved. Thus, when Sherman went too far in his negotiations with Joe Johnston for surrender of that army, Halleck issued orders that Sherman's orders should not be obeyed. When Halleck, regretting this action, tried to reconcile with Sherman, he was rebuffed.

After the war Halleck continued in the army, but was shunted aside for the most part into far-flung administrative positions.

(Below is a clearly stylized image of Halleck as a young, vital, and vibrant military commander):

Further Reading: John F. Marszalek, *Commander of All Lincoln's Armies: A Life of Henry W. Halleck.* Harvard University Press, 2004; Curt Anders, *Henry Halleck's War: A Fresh Look at Lincoln's Controversial General-in-Chief.* Guild Press of Indiana, 1999.

John Bell Hood, Warrior

John Bell Hood and the Peter Principle

When Sherman learned that Hood had replaced Joseph Johnston as commander of the Army of Tennessee in July 1864 in the middle the Atlanta campaign, he asked his subordinates, many of whom knew Hood from West Point, their opinions of the man. John Schofield said he was "bold even to rashness and courageous in the extreme." O.O. Howard said later, acerbically, "he is a stupid fellow but a hard fighter - does some very unexpected things." The consensus was that Hood would be aggressive and attack rather than use the Fabian, defensive-oriented tactics Johnston had effectively implemented until then.

Union General Jacob Cox, the deputy commander of the Army of the Ohio during the Atlanta campaign, later commented in his memoirs, "The change of commanders undoubtedly precipitated the ruin of the Confederate cause…We regarded the removal of Johnston as equivalent of a victory for us…The actions of the Confederate government was a confession that Sherman's methods had brought about the very result he aimed at."

What Cox meant was that Union soldiers had become so skilled at setting up breastworks and defenses that any offensive-oriented approach was sure to fail. A few days after taking command, Hood issued a statement to his men stating, "SOLDIERS: Experience has proved to you that safety in time of battle consists in getting into close quarters with your enemy." That signaled that he was going to be aggressive and offensive-oriented. It would be his downfall.

Most historian agree that Hood was a superb fighter and leader up to and including the corps level. On the Peninsula, at Antietam, at Gettysburg, and at Chickamauga, his inspired leadership brought his troops significant advances. It also brought Hood major injuries, which severely limited his physical mobility. He had to be strapped onto his horse during his later campaigns.

Hood was ambitious, and during the Atlanta campaign, prompted by Jefferson Davis, he had sent Davis critiques of Johnston's performance. In these letters he did not include reference to his own failings, e.g. at Cassville, which led to a retreat by Johnston at Hood's recommendation. Hood also underlined that, unlike Johnston, he would be aggressive, and that turned the trick for Davis, who in any case disliked Johnston intensely.

During the Franklin-Nashville campaign in late 1864 Hood proved the validity of the "Peter Principle." This concept, posited by Laurence Peter in 1969, states that in any organization a person rises until he reaches his "level of incompetence." While the book was a satire, the concept remains valid.

During the campaign Hood made several mistakes, while blaming his subordinates for any and all problems his army experienced. At the Battle of Spring Hill, after declaring he would personally lead the assault, he changed his orders repeatedly. This ultimately let the entire Union army pass by his troops under cover of night. At Franklin he did no reconnaissance of the Union lines and focused his attacks on the strongest breastworks. He did not give Nathan Bedford Forrest the infantry support he needed for a flank attack which had some chance of success. Finally, Hood continued attacking into the night when there was no chance of success. That debilitated his army, in which many senior officers would be killed or seriously wounded.

While his situation was hopeless after Franklin, Hood plunged on, and his performance at the Battle of Nashville only worsened the situation. At one point he weakened his army by sending Forrest to Murfreesboro to attack the garrison there, for no obvious reason. Having called defensive-oriented fighting "evil," he put his men into a defensive position outside Nashville and dared George Thomas to attack. He did, on a day Forrest was away, and by late December 16, for the first and only time in the Civil War, an entire army was fundamentally destroyed. Hood resigned soon afterward, and he received no further orders.

(Below is a banner issued 30 years later of Confederate "heroes," including Hood).

Further Reading: Brian Craig Miller, *John Bell Hood and the Fight for Civil War Memory*, Knoxville: University of Tennessee Press, 2010; Richard M. McMurray, *John Bell Hood and the War for Southern Independence.* Lexington: University Press of Kentucky, 1982

"Fighting" (?) Joe Hooker

Joe Hooker, Troublemaker Par Excellence

Lincoln's order giving Hooker command of the Army of the Potomac on January 26, 1863 is one of the strangest examples of its kind. It is also a superb example of the degree to which Abraham Lincoln was an excellent judge of people, especially someone like the much-disliked and overtly-ambitious Hooker. It read in part:

"GENERAL: I have placed you at the head of the Army of the Potomac. Of course I have done this upon what appears to me to be sufficient reasons, and yet I think it best for you to know that there are some things in regard to which I am not quite satisfied with you. I believe you to be a brave and skillful soldier, which, of course, I like…You are ambitious, which, within reasonable bounds, does good rather than harm; but I think that during General Burnside's command of the army, you have taken counsel of your ambition, and thwarted him as much as you could, in which you did a great wrong to the country and to a most meritorious and honorable brother officer. I have heard, in such a way as to believe it, of your recently saying that both the Army and the Government needed a dictator… What I now ask of you is military success, and I will risk the dictatorship…I much fear that the spirit which you have aided to infuse into the army, of criticizing their commander and withholding confidence from him, will now turn upon you… And now beware of rashness…go forth and bring us victories."

Allegedly, when Hooker received this order, he said that while he was somewhat chagrined, he was also was touched by its tone of mingled authority and kindness, stating, "He talks to me like a father…I shall not answer this letter until I have given him a great victory." Hooker never responded to the letter because he never gave Lincoln a great victory.

Joe Hooker might be described as a Machiavellian who talked too much. While he intrigued behind the scenes to gain positions for himself, he also often told the press and other generals of his ambitions and what he thought of Lincoln, Stanton, and his rivals. For example, just before the Battle of Antietam, Hooker was given significant new responsibilities while the roles of two of other senior generals, Ambrose Burnside and Edwin Sumner, were diminished. Hooker had performed well under McClellan during the Peninsula campaign. He apparently used that and exaggerations about his role at the Battle of South Mountain to persuade McClellan to make the change. It should not have been surprising then that later Burnside accepted command of the Army of the Potomac only because he knew Hooker was the alternative.

In many ways Hooker and McClellan had similar attributes. Both were excellent at training and preparing their armies. Although he wasn't "loved" by his men, as McClellan was, Hooker's men came to know that he had their interests at heart. His reforms after the disastrous Battle of Fredericksburg were critical to enhancing morale in the Army of the Potomac.

On the battlefield too the two men had similarities. Neither had the proverbial "killer instinct." At Antietam McClellan let numerous opportunities to destroy Lee's Army of Northern Virginia slip out of his hand. Even after Lincoln told him to "destroy the enemy army," he seems to have been aiming only for a limited victory.

As for Hooker, he boasted that he would win a great victory after succeeding Burnside, and his plan for the Chancellorsville campaign was brilliant. However, he delayed implementing it, even as Lee gambled and won by smashing Hooker's right wing. Hooker then limped away, unwilling to listen to subordinates who could see that the Union army still had the opportunity to destroy Lee's army.

To give him credit, after being sent West in semi-disgrace, Hooker performed well for a time, leading a Union victory at Lookout Mountain outside Chattanooga. He also was a dutiful subordinate to George Thomas during the Atlanta campaign. But when he was denied a senior command after the death of James McPherson, commander of the Army of the Tennessee, he left the army rather than do his assigned duties. He likely knew that he did not get that command because his of reputation.

It should be noted that the term "Hooker" as a synonym for a prostitute pre-dated Hooker's appearance on the public stage. On the other hand, Hooker's camps always had the reputation for being hotbeds of gambling, drinking, and loose ladies.

Robert E. Lee did not often state his opinions of his opposite numbers, but he did say that he looked forward to defeating "Mr. Fighting Joe

Hooker." In doing so he reflected his distaste for Hooker's boastful manner and also his nickname. The latter was the result of a typo in a newspaper article, but Hooker was stuck with it throughout his military career. In truth, he was very much a fighter, but not always against the eclared enemy.

(Below is a stylized image of Hooker on horseback).

Further Reading: Walter H. Hebert, *Fighting Joe Hooker,* Lincoln: University of Nebraska Press, 1944; John H. and David Eicher, *Civil War High Commands.* Stanford: Stanford University Press, 2001.

Alvin Hovey, The Ultimate Lobbyist

Alvin Hovey: Addition by Subtraction

In a long and honorable public career during which Hovey was an Indiana Supreme Court Justice, Governor of Indiana, and a congressman, Alvin Hovey is best known in Civil War history for one significant misjudgment. His negative actions during the Atlanta campaign caught the attention of William T. Sherman and Abraham Lincoln and damaged the image of Political Generals.

Hovey was a Justice in the Indiana Supreme Court at the age of 34 and U.S. Attorney for Indiana at 35. He began the Civil War as a Colonel in the Indiana militia, and after effective service at Shiloh, Corinth, and Vicksburg, he became a Brigadier General of Volunteers. Grant was so pleased by Hovey's service at Vicksburg that he arranged for him to be a division commander in John Schofield's 23rd corps for the Atlanta campaign in 1864.

Not long before he took up that position, Hovey's wife died. It is possible that his inevitable sadness may had led to an emotional breakdown. Within weeks of the beginning of the Atlanta campaign, Schofield petitioned Sherman to have Hovey removed. Schofield wrote that Hovey was "utterly inefficient and worthless as a division commander," adding that he seemed to have "some sort of mental disease." Sherman resisted because Grant had specifically made the appointment. Eventually, after Schofield told Sherman, "I dare not trust him in the handling of the troops," he accepted Hovey's resignation on June 8.

At the time, tendering a resignation in the presence of the enemy was usually a cause for summary dismissal. But Hovey, who had powerful friends in Grant and Indiana Governor Oliver P. Morton, let it be known that he was going to go to Washington to try to get a promotion. Meanwhile, Schofield reorganized his troops, and through "addition by subtraction," i.e. without Hovey hindering him, he now had solid and reliable subordinate leadership.

Hovey's troublemaking caused another furor in the campaign when news came in early July that he had, in fact, gained a promotion to Major General. Jacob Cox, his fellow division commander, fumed in a letter home,

"This is a wanton insult to the whole army..[that] this skulker is made a Major General." Sherman too was enraged, writing Halleck that the promotion was "an act of injustice...if the rear be the post of honor, then we had all better change front on Washington."

Sherman was astounded then on July 26 to get a message from Lincoln, who tried to calm the storm. The President said he understood Sherman's unhappiness, but promised that worthy generals would gain promotions after the campaign. Sherman distributed Lincoln's response, which enhanced morale.

After getting his promotion, Hovey got no new combat assignments, spending the rest of the war in administrative duty in Indiana. He was U.S. Minister to Peru from 1865 to 1870, served one term in Congress, and was Indiana's Governor from 1888 until his death in 1891.

(Below is an image of Hovey's powerful patron, Indiana Governor Oliver P. Morton).

Further Reading: Linda Gugin and James St. Clair, eds., *The Governors of Indiana.* Indianapolis: Indiana Historical Society Press, 2006; Ezra J. Warner, *Generals in Blue.* Baton Rouge: LSU Press, 1964; Eugene D. Schmiel, *Citizen-General: Jacob Dolson Cox and the Civil War Era*, Athens: Ohio University Press, 2014.

Henry J.Hunt, Artilleryist

Henry Jackson Hunt and Pickett's Charge

The question as to whether the Civil War was the first "modern" war because it introduced so many more efficient ways to kill the enemy continues to be debated. Repeater rifles and Gatling guns are often mentioned as key innovations, but in fact they played only a small role. On the other hand, innovations in the artillery, from "payload" to distance capability were essential to devastation in the Civil War. The third day at the Battle of Gettysburg exhibited a prime example, when the skills of Army of the Potomac artillery commander Henry Hunt helped lead to Union victory.

Hunt graduated from West Point in 1839 and joined the artillery corps. He fought in Mexico and was one of the authors of the 1856 army artillery manual. He performed well at First Manassas and Malvern Hill, and was named to head the army's artillery just before the Battle of Antietam. There his cannons did yeoman work against the Confederates.

At Gettysburg on July 3, 1863, Union commander George Meade believed that Confederate commander Robert E. Lee would engage in a frontal attack, In response he ordered creation of a strong defensive line, including massive artillery under Hunt's command. That morning Hunt did a visual reconnaissance of the Confederate line and determined that in fact a major infantry attack, preceded by an immense artillery bombardment, was imminent.

At 1 PM the Confederates began what would be a two-hour long artillery barrage on the Union line. Wisely, and because Meade had given him significant autonomy, Hunt resisted suggestions to engage in an artillery duel, though other senior generals did expend some of their long-range shells. For his part, Hunt used a variety of subterfuges to convince the Confederates that they had knocked out the Union artillery. In fact he had conserved most of his capabilities for the ensuing infantry rush.

As a result, when the Confederate infantry moved to attack, they were met with not only significant rifle fire, but also an artillery cannonade of a breadth perhaps never before seen in combat. (see below for a posed image of a cannon and cannoneers at Gettysburg). Artillery shells and canister ripped the rebel lines to shreds, resulting in casualties ranging up to

70% in some regiments. Hunt conjectured later in an article in *Battles and Leaders of the Civil War* that he would have wiped out the charging infantry even earlier if he had been able to convince his fellow commanders to withhold all of the cannonade. We will never know, but it is certain that Henry Jackson Hunt's tactical skill was triumphant that day. His understanding of the most effective use of artillery made him a true trailblazer.

Hunt served with Meade and the Army of the Potomac for the rest of the war, but the artillery was not as needed – or as effective – as it was at Gettysburg. But with his brilliant plan and attack at Gettysburg, Hunt's standing as the greatest Artilleryist of the Union army was secure.

Further Reading: Edward G. Longacre, *The Man Behind the Guns: A Military Biography of General Henry J. Hunt*. South Brunswick, NJ: A.S. Barnes, 1977; David and John H. Eicher, *Civil War High Commands*. Stanford, CA: Stanford University Press, 2001.

Andrew Johnson, Lincoln's Worst Decision

Andrew Johnson and 150 Years of Conflict

The inevitable concern about the fate of the nation following the tragedy of Lincoln's assassination was diminished by the belief in Washington that Vice President Andrew Johnson would follow Lincoln's policy on Reconstruction. Johnson's drunkenness at the inauguration was put aside in the hope that the dignity of his new office would make him a better man and a true leader.

Those hopes proved to be in vain. Johnson proceeded to move rapidly from his previous commitment to a "hard" Reconstruction to declaring the war over, pardoning almost every rebel, and ignoring or dismissing abuses against freedmen in the defeated states.

As one of his strongest supporters before he changed his policies, Governor of Ohio Jacob Cox, wrote in 1866,

"Johnson has disappointed everybody: the Democrats who adopted hm as well as the Republicans whom he abandoned." Calling Johnson a "failure and a cipher," an embittered Cox said he had stayed as loyal as long as he did only to protect against the kind of Reconstruction that no one could accept. Cox wrote acerbically of Johnson, "he is obstinate without being firm, self-opinionated without being capable of systematic thinking, combative and pugnacious without being courageous...The Democracy played with him as an angler with a trout," and their Southern allies, who had "always looked down upon him as a 'mean white,' puffed him with the idea that he was to be the leader of their class of Southern gentlemen."

Johnson was a typical choice for Vice President in that era. There was little or no concern about the possibility of his ever becoming president, and he was rewarded for being the only loyal governor from the South. Lincoln played almost no role in the choice, but accepted it as a reasonable political decision which would help in his re-election, which it did.

Retired diplomat Chas. Freeman's book on statecraft, *Arts of Power*, posits, "The motive of war is to compel an enemy to agree to or to acquiesce in terms and conditions it would not otherwise accept. If victory does not produce this result, the sacrifices required to produce victory are in vain...A humbled adversary must be brought to regard the concessions defeat imposes as final, and not subject to later revision or reversal."

Andrew Johnson's policies resulted in the opposite of this desiderata, as the defeated Confederates slowly but surely reasserted their authority in the South. Johnson would over time allow Southern state governments to be led by former rebels, to do the absolute minimum to comply with the terms of their defeat, and to pass "Black Codes" putting freedmen into a state of quasi-slavery. Critics told him that it was almost as if the war had not been fought, and that their sacrifices to produce victory had been in vain. But Johnson, whose strongest attribute was stubbornness, would not budge.

Congressional Reconstruction, implemented primarily because of the failure of Johnson's polices was an attempt to implement a peace which justified the sacrifices the war had entailed. For a while it succeeded. But the South was by no means a "humbled adversary" as defined by Freeman. Encouraged by former leaders, including Robert E. Lee, as well as by Johnson's policies, the former Confederate states resisted in every possible way. Implicitly, looking at the "long term," the region's traditional leaders were banking on Northern reluctance to continue military occupation indefinitely and Northern indifference to the plight of the freedman. With the Compromise of 1877 and the end of military reconstruction, their gamble paid off.

The subsequent racial divisions and problems are slowly but surely being resolved, and the United States of 2020 is a far better place for people of all races than it has ever been. But the foundations for those problems were set during Reconstruction, and Andrew Johnson is perhaps more responsible than anyone else.

(Below is an image of the Senate meeting to decide if Johnson, having been impeached, should be convicted. He was not, but perhaps he should have been? That is the subject of an alternative history yet to be written).

Further Reading: Eric L. McKitrick, *Andrew Johnson and Reconstruction*, New York: Oxford University Press, 1988; Michael Les Benedict, *The Impeachment and Trial of Andrew Johnson*, New York: Norton, 1973.

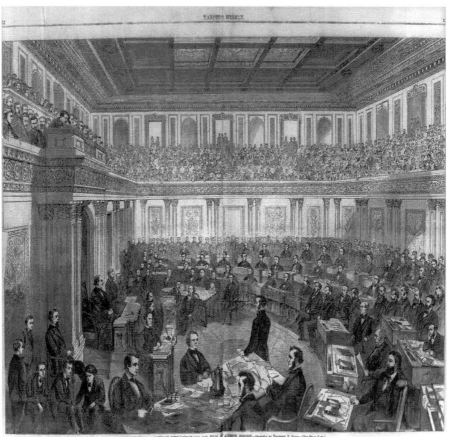

Judson Kilpatrick, "Kill Cavalry"

Judson Kilpatrick, Colorful and Effective "Damned Fool"

Looking at his picture, one might find it difficult to see "Kill Cavalry" Kilpatrick as a "ladies' man" and a hard-driving military commander. However, these quotes from other Union generals explain it all:

*"His notorious immoralities and rapacity set so demoralizing an example to his troops that the best disciplinarians among his subordinates could only mitigate its influence...the value of his services made his commander willing to be ignorant of escapades which he could hardly condone...he was quite capable of ...dare-devil recklessness that dismayed his opponents and imparted his own daring to his men." (*General Jacob Cox).

"I know that Kilpatrick is a hell of damned fool, but I want just that sort of a man to command my cavalry on this expedition." (General William T. Sherman)

Kilpatrick graduated from West Point in 1861 just as the war was beginning, and he was reportedly the first Union officer wounded, at the Battle of Big Bethel, June 10, 1861. At Second Bull Run he made his first of several foolhardy cavalry charges, losing a significant portion of his men, leading to his sobriquet, "Kill Cavalry." In 1862, further adding to his "reputation," he was arrested twice, once for selling captured goods and once for being drunk on duty.

Despite his personal problems and peccadilloes, Kilpatrick was known as a hard fighter, and he continued to get important assignments as a cavalry commander. His cavalry were the only effective element of Stoneman's raids before the Battle of Chancellorsville, reaching the outskirts of Richmond. He also performed well against JEB Stuart at Brandy Station, the largest cavalry battle of the war. On the way to Gettysburg in June 1863, however, both Stuart and Kilpatrick "lost their way," with the latter chasing the former and neither providing any useful intelligence to their commanders.

Early in 1864 Kilpatrick led a raid on Richmond during which, once again, many of his troops were killed. Ulric Dahlgren, the leader of the infantry in the raid, was killed, and documents were found on his person which allegedly stated the goal of the raid was to assassinate Jefferson Davis. The so-called Kilpatrick-Dahlgren Raid's authorizer is uncertain, but Secretary of War Edwin Stanton may have been behind it.

Afterward, Kilpatrick transferred to Sherman's command for the Atlanta campaign and March to the Sea. During the latter, he performed effectively in implementing the "hard hand of war" against the Southern economy. Perhaps not surprisingly, during that campaign he was almost taken prisoner when Confederate troops raided his headquarters where he was asleep with a lady not his wife. Kilpatrick fled in his underclothes, but went on to further duties until Johnston surrendered to Sherman.

Kilpatrick resigned from the army in late 1865, and became active in Republican politics, while also securing diplomatic positions under Johnson and Grant.

(The image below shows Kilpatrick in a cavalry raid)

Further Reading: Samuel J. Martin, *Kill-Cavalry: The Life of Union General Hugh Judson Kilpatrick.* Mechanicsburg, PA: Stackpole Books, 2000; Duane Schultz, *The Dahlgren Affair: Terror and Conspiracy in the Civil War.* New York: Norton, 1999.

COLONEL KILPATRICK'S LATE CAVALRY RAID THROUGH VIRGINIA.—[See Page 34.]

James H. Ledlie, Alcoholic

James H. Ledlie and Dereliction of Duty

The Battle of the Crater is a supreme example of good intentions and excellent planning being derailed by bureaucracy and poor decision-making. And, as on so many occasions, Ambrose Burnside was judged partly at fault because of the failures of his subordinates – but also because of his lack of oversight.

James Ledlie was the most important of those subordinates and the one most to blame. He had joined the army in 1861 after a career in New York as a civil engineer. He spent the first years of the war in the artillery corps guarding the Virginia and North Carolina coasts. He was promoted to Brigadier General in 1863.

Ledlie transferred to Burnside's IXth corps for the Overland campaign in 1864, and became commander of the 1st division in June. Despite his high rank, Ledlie had seen little fighting It appears that the vicious and bloody maelstrom of this campaign both unnerved him and drove him (perhaps further?) to drink. During the battles of Spotsylvania and North Anna he performed poorly, and some of his staff alleged he was drunk on both occasions.

Unbeknownst to Ledlie, Burnside and Grant had agreed to a proposal by a group of Pennsylvania soldiers, former coal miners, to tunnel under the Confederate lines and blow a hole in the Confederate breastworks outside Petersburg. That would be followed by a Union advance, hopefully splitting the Confederate defenses. Burnside proposed and Grant agreed that a group of U.S. Colored Troops from another division would lead the "follow up" charge.

But General George Meade interceded, fearing, he said, that if the Colored troops failed, he would be accused by antislavery Republicans of sacrificing them. Instead Burnside was ordered to choose troops from one of his other divisions, none of whom had been trained for this mission. Burnside, for reasons that remain unclear, chose from among the other divisions by drawing lots. Sadly, Ledlie's men "won" the lottery.

When the blast went off early on the morning of July 30, the ill-prepared 1st division troops charged ahead, unaccompanied by their commander, who remained in his tent, allegedly ill but certainly drunk. The Confederates lost many men in the blast, but they responded quickly and picked off many of the Union troops, many of whom were trapped at the bottom of the hole. Burnside then unwisely sent in the Colored troops in the hope they could save the day, but they too became "sitting ducks." The Confederates killed many of the black troops after they were taken prisoner.

Ledlie was criticized in an official inquiry, and he resigned his position in January 1865. His troublemaking and incompetence seemingly did not harm his postwar career, as he participated in the building of the Union Pacific railroad. In his memoirs Grant said of Ledlie, he "was otherwise inefficient, proved also to possess disqualification less common among soldiers," i.e. cowardice.

(Below is a contemporary image of "The Crater")

Further Reading: Earl Hess, *Into the Crater: The Mine Attack at Petersburg*. Columbia: University of South Carolina Press, 2010; Slotkin, Richard, *No Quarter: The Battle of the Crater, 1864*. New York: Random House, 2009.

THE BATTLE OF THE PETERSBURG CRATER.   555

THE CRATER, AS SEEN FROM THE UNION SIDE. FROM A SKETCH MADE AT THE TIME.

In October, 1887, Major James C. Coit, of Cheraw, South Carolina, wrote as follows with regard to this picture, and the Confederate battery, under his command, bear- on the day of the explosion. This battery (Wright's), where I was during the engagement, was just across the ravine to our left of the crater and just in rear of our infantry line, about

Dr. Jonathan Letterman and Staff

Jonathan Letterman, "Father of Battlefield Medicine"

Like just about everything else in the Civil War, in which no one countenanced a continental war involving millions of men, medical practitioners made it up as they went along. As in the case of nursing, photography, ballistics, strategy, and many other elements, they made vast improvements, primarily through trial and error. Dr. Jonathan Letterman, chief of surgery for the Army of the Potomac, trailblazed more medical reforms than anyone else, earning his accolade "Father of Battlefield Medicine."

After graduating from Jefferson Medical College in 1849, Letterman became an assistant surgeon in the Army Medical Department. When the war began he had significant experience dealing with the military. After joining the Army of the Potomac, Letterman was appointed its medical director. He was given *carte blanche* by commanding General George McClellan to improve a system which had made almost no organized system for the care of thousands of wounded and dying men.

Of the many advances in medical care which Dr. Letterman pioneered by the time of the Battle of Antietam, the bloodiest one day battle in American history, were triage of cases, an efficient ambulance system, and the modern field hospital. He also instituted an efficient system for the control and distribution of medical supplies. His innovations, which saved hundreds of lives when they were implemented after the Battle of Gettysburg, became standard procedure by an Act of Congress in 1864.

Sadly, Dr. Letterman's contributions were not sufficiently understood or appreciated at the time, and by early 1864 he was no longer part of the Army of the Potomac. He resigned from the army in December that year. He wrote his memoirs about his military experiences in 1866, and eventually he was recognized for the revolution he had instituted in medical care.

(Below is an image of medical care from "Harper's Weekly"):

Further Reading: Scott McGaugh, *Surgeon in Blue: Joseph Letterman, the Civil War Doctor Who Pioneered Battlefield Care.* New York: Simon and Schuster, 2013; Jonathan Letterman, *Medical Recollections of the Army of the Potomac.* New York, G.P. Putnam, 1866.

Abraham Lincoln, "Political General"

Abraham Lincoln, Visionary Military Man

The Civil War revolutionized the American army and military practice in many ways. The ascendancy of the professional soldier to all command positions was accompanied by a realization that "citizen-soldiers" and Political Generals were critical to victory at a time when 98% of the army was made up of volunteers. While there were many successful Political Generals like John Logan, Joshua Chamberlain, and Jacob Cox, by far the most talented Union Political General was Abraham Lincoln.

Much of the Union war effort was improvised because no one, not even General-in-Chief Winfield Scott, envisioned a continental war in which millions would fight and over 700,000 would die. Many, including in his Cabinet, thought of Lincoln as a country bumpkin at first. But he proved to be a quick study in every aspect of decision-making at the presidential level, including fomenting and managing war.

Over time, Lincoln gained a solid understanding of military strategy and, despite making some major mistakes, often understood the best approach to military situations sooner than his military leaders. As esteemed historian James McPherson has written, Lincoln came implicitly to understand Clausewitz's view that "The political objective is the goal, war is the means of reaching it, and means can never be considered in isolation from their purpose. Therefore, it is clear that war should never be thought of as *something autonomous* but always as an instrument of policy."

Perhaps Lincoln's most important political-military decision was to implement a "hard hand of war" policy in 1862. That included issuing the Emancipation Proclamation and ordering the creation of black regiments. Early on, unlike many of his generals, he concluded that victory would come by defeating Confederate armies, not by taking their cities or pushing them back from Northern invasions.

One of the best examples of this divergence of viewpoints came after Union victory at the Battle of South Mountain, September 14, 1862. Lincoln wrote to Union commander George McClellan, "God bless you, and all with you; destroy the rebel army if possible." Instead McClellan only achieved a tactical victory a few days later at Antietam while missing several opportunities to destroy Lee's army. Afterward, McClellan reported that he had achieved "complete victory...the enemy is driven back into Virginia. Maryland and Penna. are now safe."

Another example of Lincoln's intensive study of military literature came after the Maryland campaign. At a time when McClellan's forces were closer to Richmond than Lee's, Lincoln advised him, using military terminology, that his advantage was because he held "the interior line." McClellan saw this as Lincoln's further "interfering" in military matters.

In 1863, when Lee was advancing into Pennsylvania toward Gettysburg, Army of the Potomac Commander Joe Hooker told Lincoln that this provided a great opportunity to seize Richmond. Lincoln responded, "Lee's army, and not Richmond, is your true objective point." When Meade, after his victory at Gettysburg, praised his army's driving the enemy "from our soil," Lincoln complained that generals did not understand that "the whole country is our soil."

After Grant and Sherman, two men who understood the need to destroy the rebel armies, took command in 1864, Lincoln became less involved in making policy or directing actions. (see image below). When Grant issued, in April 1864, the first comprehensive national military strategy, one focused on multiple attacks on multiple armies, Lincoln's statement, "Grant is my man, and I am his the rest of the war" was apt. After trial and error on many fronts, Lincoln had found generals who understood how to win – and they did.

Esteemed scholar T. Harry Williams wrote the following about Lincoln as a military leader: *"Lincoln stands out as a great war president, probably the greatest in our history, and a great natural strategist, a better one than any of his generals. He was in actuality as well as in title the commander in chief who, by his larger strategy, did more than Grant or any general to win the war for the Union."*

Further Reading: Thomas J. Goss, *The War within the Union High Command; Politics and Generalship during the Civil War.* Lawrence: University Press of Kansas, 2003; and T. Harry Williams, *Lincoln and His Generals.* New York: Random House, 2011 edition.

Chapter IV: *Creativity and Military Blindness*

This group includes innovators, inventors, and incompetents.

Dr. Thaddeus Lowe (1832-1913) and his observations balloons were an innovation which the Union army failed to utilize sufficiently.

Union General **Montgomery Meigs** (1816-1892) was the greatest "unsung hero" of the Union because of his masterful command of logistics.

Union General **Dixon Miles** (1804-1862) lost his command at Harpers Ferry through indecision, bad judgments, and too much alcohol.

Union General **Robert Milroy** (1816-1890) was a failure at nearly every campaign, yet continued to gain promotions.

Confederate General **John Mosby** (1833-1916) was a "raider" who successfully utilized unconventional tactics to frustrate the Union war effort.

Thomas Nast (1840-1902) was a crusading political cartoonist for the influential *Harpers Weekly.*

Confederate General **John Pemberton**, (1814-1881) who surrendered Vicksburg, was always suspect because he came from Pennsylvania.

Confederate General **George Pickett** (1825-1875) played only a small role in the charge named after him, and his inattention while on duty was a critical reason for Lee's retreat from Petersburg.

Union General **John Pope** (1822-1892) talked a good game, but his multiple mistakes at the Battle of Second Manassas opened the way for Lee's first invasion of the North.

Union General **Fitz-John Porter** (1822-1901) was cashiered from the army for his mistakes at Second Bull Run and for his political allegiance to the Democratic Party.

Thaddeus Lowe, Above it All

Thaddeus Lowe, and the Loss of an Asset

The analysis by historians of the problems resulting from the conservatism of the Ordnance Department of both the Union and Confederate armies usually focuses on resistance to new weapons such as the repeater rifle and Gatling Gun. The observation balloon certainly belongs in that group as an obviously-useful weapon that most generals refused to use or even to consider.

Thaddeus Lowe, a self-taught scientist and inventor, was one of several young Americans who had been experimenting with balloon travel in the 1850's. When the Civil War began, he used influential friends to contact Secretary of the Treasury Salmon Chase to suggest that observation balloons be used by the army. In a June 1861 experiment his balloon "Enterprise" not only observed Washington from 500 feet, but also transmitted a telegraphed message using wires strung to the ground. Lincoln was convinced of its value, and Lowe was named head of the "Balloon Corps," though that group was not within the military structure.

Lowe constructed several balloons complete with a system of generators which could be moved as needed, depending on military necessity. He first tested one in September 1861 under the command of General Fitz-John Porter, who successfully spotted previously-unknown Confederate gun-sites, which were then attacked. He and his balloons were active during McClellan's Peninsula campaign, gathering essential intelligence. The balloons were able to be placed far enough away that they could not be hit by Confederate artillery. One of the volunteers to go up in a balloon during this campaign was a particularly-audacious young Captain on McClellan's staff named George Custer.

Despite his successes, Lowe was beset by attacks from rival aeronauts and bureaucratic military men intent on saving money. Also, he apparently had not convinced even the sympathetic McClellan of the efficacy of balloons. In a letter to his wife in April 1862, McClellan noted that his colleague General Fitz-John Porter had gone up in a balloon and had almost landed behind enemy lines. McClellan wrote, "You may rest assured of one thing: you won't catch me in the confounded balloon nor will I allow any other Generals to go up in it!" A downtrodden Lowe said of this experience, "I found it difficult for a time to restore confidence among the officers as to the safety of this means of observation on account of this accident." (Sears, *The Civil War Papers of George McClellan*).

Lowe's final contribution to the military effort was at Fredericksburg when Ambrose Burnside asked him to discern the whereabouts of his deputy William Franklin (see above) at a critical moment. Unfortunately, he found that Franklin, as usual, was barely moving, a key to the Union defeat.

Disgusted by the lack of support and the decision to move the Balloon Corps to the Engineer Corps, Lowe resigned in May 1863. The Balloon Corps was disbanded that August, this potentially-valuable asset figuratively put into the Orwellian memory hole.

(Below is an image of soldiers launching one of Lowe's balloons during the Peninsula campaign).

Further Reading: Michael Jaeger and Carol Lauritzen, eds., *Memoirs of Thaddeus S.C. Lowe*, Edwin Menton Printers, 2004; Charles Evans, *War of the Aeronauts*. Stackpole Books, 2002.

Montgomery Meigs, the Unsung Hero

Montgomery Meigs and the Well-Fed Army

There are many "unsung heroes" on both sides of the Civil War, but none was more important than Montgomery Meigs. The Union army was better-fed, better-armed, and better-equipped for battle than the Confederates, primarily due to this master of logistics, the Quartermaster General of the army.

Born into a prosperous family, Meigs graduated from West Point in 1836. He spent most of his years before the Civil War engaged in engineering, including once assisting Robert E. Lee in improving navigation of the Mississippi River. He created the Washington Aqueduct and was supervising the building of the dome and new wings of the Capitol building before war broke out.

These projects made him well known in Washington for his engineering and organizational skills and made him a natural choice to replace Joseph Johnston as Quartermaster General in May 1861. Meigs rapidly systematized the procurement of good and services and the movement of supplies, from food to weapons. The contrast with the Confederate system was never more evident than when a typical soldier sat down to eat – Billy Yank almost always had three good meals a day – Johnny Reb almost always was foraging and eating whatever he could find along the way.

Although the parallel is inexact, Meigs and General George Marshall were great military men although neither were involved in combat in their wars, the Civil War and World War II. Trained as military officers, each wanted to be out on the field fighting. But their presidents determined that they were more important behind the scenes, playing critical roles which no one had performed better.

After the war Meigs focused on several projects, one of the most important of which he had begun in 1864 by choosing Robert E. Lee's estate in Arlington as the site of a military cemetery. He designed many elements of the graveyard, including the Civil War Unknowns Monument, He deliberately placed that edifice near to the Lee-Custis mansion to underline his distaste for Lee's having turned his back on the Union.

His other major project was construction of the Pension building, required because of the vast number of Civil War pensions. The red brick building is now the National Building museum, but its original design includes an extensive bas relief of Civil War soldiers.

(Below is an image from the bas relief on the Pension building)

Further Reading: Robert O'Harrow, *The Quartermaster: Montgomery C. Meigs, Lincoln's General, Master Builder of the Union Army.* New York: Simon and Schuster, 2016; David W. Miller, *Second Only to Grant: Quartermaster General Montgomery C. Meigs.* White Mane Publishing 2001.:

Dixon Miles, Out of Place at Harpers Ferry

Miles's Many Mistakes

When Civil War generals committed significant mistakes during combat, they were often "punished" by being assigned to "backwater" posts. Two high-ranking Union generals in that category were William Rosecrans and John Pope. Rosecrans's defeat at Chickamauga was followed by his assignment to administrative duty. Pope's defeat at Second Manassas led to his assignment fighting the Sioux Indians. Neither man was given a new combat assignment, though Pope remained in the army.

Another senior officer "punished" in this way was Colonel Dixon Miles. He was a West Point graduate (1824) and regular army officer who commanded a reserve division during the Battle of First Manassas, July 21, 1861. Although Miles and his men played only a small role that day, he was charged with being drunk on duty. The charge was confirmed, and after a leave of absence, Miles was shuffled aside. He was now commander in the backwater of Harpers Ferry, where he would be in charge of the arsenal and some 10,000 men. Then the "law of unintended consequences" kicked in.

The arsenal and the town were well-known at the time because of John Brown's raid in 1859. The fact that Brown saw it as a potentially-easy target is not surprising. Harpers Ferry is situated in a beautiful spot at the bottom of a peninsula formed by the Shenandoah and Potomac Rivers. It is surrounded on all sides by high hills. While a wise commander of the city could take steps to defend it by stationing men on the surrounding heights, the city would still remain a proverbial "sitting duck."

In September 1862 Robert E. Lee, fresh from his victory at Second Manassas, invaded Maryland. George McClellan, commanding the Union forces, saw Harpers Ferry as a likely target for Lee. He pleaded with District Commander General John Wool and General-in-Chief Henry Halleck to abandon the city and send Miles's forces to join his Army of the Potomac. Halleck resisted until it was too late, and on September 9 Lee sent three sets of his men to surround and take Harpers Ferry.

As the Confederates approached, Colonel Miles dithered. Not sure what to do, he set up defenses to his north on the mainland, but quixotically removed troops which had been stationed on Maryland Heights (from which

John Brown had launched his attack) and brought them back into the city. As for Loudoun Heights, the other hill which commanded a view of the city, Miles determined that no force would be able to climb them or be a threat. He would be wrong.

By September 14 the Confederates had the city surrounded, including on both heights. The next day Miles held a council of war and he decided to surrender. Many of his officers were disgusted with his actions, and some later accused him of being drunk during this period. One cavalry division commander ignored Miles's orders and escaped to the north (see image below), later successfully disrupting Confederate General James Longstreet's supply train.

The Confederates were bombing the city on September 15 when the white flag of surrender was seen. Unfortunately for Miles, he was killed during the bombardment. Some 12,000 men surrendered. Two days later Confederate General A.P. Hill moved north from Harpers Ferry to attack the Union at the Battle of Antietam. Had Hill not arrived when he did, it is likely the Union would have destroyed Lee's army that day.

A court of inquiry into the surrender denounced Miles for "incapacity, amounting to almost imbecility." On the other hand, neither Halleck nor Wool were found to be negligent, a decision which flies in the face of the facts. Why they did not heed McClellan's sensible recommendation is unclear, but the animosity between Halleck and McClellan was likely a significant factor. As for Miles, the judgment of history is that he was one of the great failures of the war.

Further Reading: Paul R. Teetor, *A Matter of Hours: Treason at Harpers Ferry*. Fairleigh Dickinson University Press, 1982; and Chester G. Hearn, *Six Years of Hell: Harpers Ferry during the Civil War*. Baton Rouge: LSU Press, 1999.

Robert Milroy, Incompetent Rising

Robert Milroy, Failure at Every Level

Robert E. Lee's second invasion of the North in 1863 was preceded by the Second Battle of Winchester, a victory which opened the way for him to move toward Gettysburg. The Union commander at Winchester, Robert Milroy, performed poorly, as he had many times before during the war.

As one of his previous commanders, Jacob Cox, wrote contemporaneously to his wife about Milroy and this battle:

"You will recollect that my greatest chagrin at the injustice done me last Spring was that Milroy, my subordinate, was promoted over my head, without merit, ability, or military character. The recent disaster at Winchester turns out to be chargeable wholly to him, with all the train of evil consequences. He made a most disgraceful flight as I predicted he would do. No one who had known him in the field would have expected anything else. His fall has been more rapid than I looked for, but I felt sure it must come, & that the country would pay sorely for his ill-judged advancement."

Milroy began the war as a Captain in the Indiana militia, and he was made a Brigadier General of Volunteers after serving in western Virginia in 1861. During that time he gained a reputation for losing control of himself during the stress of battle. He also implemented harsh treatment of suspected Confederate sympathizers, which hampered Union attempts to gain supporters as West Virginia moved toward statehood.

Milroy performed adequately under Fremont during the 1862 Shenandoah campaign. But during a critical moment at the Second Battle of Manassas, August 30, 1862, he lost control of his emotions. Having defended well against the onslaught of the Union left by James Longstreet, Milroy suddenly left his troops and sought help from General Irvin McDowell. Apparently Milroy was so overcome with emotion at that critical moment that he could only babble incomprehensibly. McDowell later reported he seemed to be "in a state of mind as unfit to judge of events." Oddly – though this happened all too frequently in the Civil War -- Milroy was promoted to Major General soon afterward.

Milroy's failure at Second Winchester, when his bravado caused his men to be overwhelmed, led to his court-martial. Though he was inexplicably declared not culpable, he was not given any further combat assignments. Though the negative reputation of Political Generals mainly reflects the failures of prominent men like Ben Butler and John C. Fremont, Milroy's performance only added to the dismal, stereotyped image.

(Below is an image of Second Manassas):

Further Reading: Jonathan Noyalas, *"My Word is Absolute Law:" A Biography of Union General Robert Milroy.* New York: McFarland, 2006; Eric Wittenberg and Scott Mingus, Sr. *The Second Battle of Winchester: The Confederate Victory that Opened the Door to Gettysburg.* Savas-Beatie, 2016.

John Mosby, Raider/Ranger

John Mosby and the Edge of Legality

As of 2020 there were over 30 markers or monuments, several schools, and a Virginia state highway memorializing John Mosby. He was a Confederate "raider" whose unorthodox and violent attacks forced the Union to devote an inordinate amount of resources to protect against him. In 1992 he was inducted into the U.S. Army Ranger Hall of Fame. As in the case of U.S. Army forts Hood, Bragg, Lee, and A.P. Hill, the United States may be the only nation that honors those who fought against the national government in this manner.

Mosby began his "public career" in 1850 when he was convicted of shooting another student at the University of Virginia. He was later pardoned and became a lawyer in Bristol, Virginia. During the secession crisis, he spoke out against it, but when Virginia seceded, Mosby joined the Confederacy. His first assignment was with a cavalry unit, the Washington Mounted Rifles, commanded by the aptly-named William "Grumble" Jones. That group was folded into the 1st Virginia Cavalry Regiment, headed by JEB Stuart, and the latter and Mosby soon began their close military relationship.

Early in 1862 Stuart began to use Mosby and his men as scouts, and they were instrumental in paving the way for Stuart's "ride around" McClellan's Union forces during the Peninsula campaign. Mosby planned to engage in raids against John Pope when the latter took command in mid-1862, but he was captured and held for three weeks before being released. Mosby then provided valuable services to Stuart and Lee during the Second Manassas and Maryland campaigns.

In late 1862 Mosby was given autonomy to conduct his raids. To do so, he recruited men from around Middleburg, Virginia, and they were christened, "Mosby's Rangers." That group spent the first half of 1863 in a series of rapidly-mobile raids against Union forces and supplies in northern Virginia, even capturing a Union general in March. They continued to successfully harass the Union forces even after Mosby was wounded twice, once in August 1863 and once in September 1864. He recovered quickly both times.

After six of his men were captured and executed because they were out of uniform, i.e. considered to be spies, Mosby took his controversial revenge. On November 6, 1864, in Rectortown, Virginia, one year after McClellan had been replaced in the same area, Mosby held a "raffle." He ordered seven Union prisoners, chosen by lot from among the group, to be executed. After Lee surrendered in April 1865 Mosby disbanded his rangers at a location about three miles from his "raffle." (see the placard below).

When the war ended, Mosby was only 31. He returned to the practice of law, and in 1872 was Grant's campaign manager in Virginia. Now active in Republican politics despite the opprobrium this brought him, he was appointed Consul to Hong Kong from 1878 to1885, and he later received a variety of minor federal positions. Mosby wrote two memoirs of his war experiences, *Mosby's War Reminiscences* and *Stuart's Cavalry Campaigns*.

Further Reading: James A. Ramage, *Gray Ghost: The Life of Col. John Singleton Mosby.* Lexington: University of Kentucky Press, 1999; Paul Ashdown and Edward Caudill. *The Mosby Myth: A Confederate Hero in Life and Legend.* Wilmington, DE: Scholarly Resources, Inc., 2002.

Thomas Nast, Trailblazing Political Cartoonist

Thomas Nast and the Power of the Pen (and Ink)

The stereotype of a picture being worth a thousand words was never truer than when readers opened the pages of *Harpers Weekly* during the Civil War era. There they would see the trailblazing political cartoons of German immigrant Thomas Nast which incisively chronicled the evolving war and American society as a whole. Also, his drawings of "Santa Claus" and "Uncle Sam" were the foundation of popular images of those iconic figures

Nast joined *Harpers* in 1862, and, firmly pro-Union, he sketched a wide variety of military-related themes. One source quoted Lincoln as saying that Nast was his best "recruiting sergeant." Nast sketched battlefields at times, but he tended to emphasize the human element of conflict. His sentimental drawing in 1862 of side-by-side images of a family praying for a soldier and the soldier prayerfully remembering his family was a particularly-effective representation of reality.

Nast's anti-Confederate views were prominent in his drawings. His images of Confederate guerrilla atrocities in the West and a two-section drawing comparing Jefferson Davis in prison and the Union soldiers at the Andersonville prison camp were particularly cutting. In 1863 he did a large drawing entitled, ""Historic Examples of Southern Chivalry – Dedicated to Jeff. Davis," showing Confederates committing a variety of atrocities (below).

A firm opponent of slavery, Nast praised Lincoln for issuing the Emancipation Proclamation, and he became an advocate of equal rights. Not surprisingly, during Reconstruction Nast was severely critical of Andrew Johnson's policies and, later, the rise of the Klux Klan.

Later, Nast became famous for his caricatures, especially of Boss Tweed and the Tammany Hall machine in New York City. Nast's cartoons are credited by some as being a critical factor in Tweed's ultimate arrest for corruption.

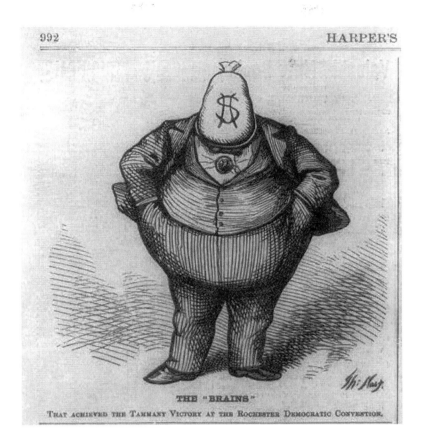

Thomas Nast's legacy as the first significant political cartoonist goes on, even as print newspapers disappear. For good or ill, the internet is rife with thousands of cartoons, memes, caricatures, and other depictions of political and societal leaders.

Further Reading: Fiona Deans Halloran, *Thomas Nast: The Father of Modern Political Cartoons*. Chapel Hill, NC: The University of North Carolina Press, 2012; Donald Dewey, *The Art of Ill Will: The Story of American Political Cartoons*. NYU Press, 2007.

John C. Pemberton, a Man In-Between

John Pemberton, Union Turncoat, Rebel Scapegoat

While both sides of the Civil War welcomed the allegiance of senior military officers from "the other side," there was on occasion a concern about the officer's true loyalties. In no case was that truer than of John C. Pemberton, Pennsylvanian turned Confederate General.

Pemberton ranked in the middle of his West Point class of 1837, and he stayed in the army until the Civil War. He served in the Seminole and Mexican wars, but mainly as a staff officer. His biographer avers that during this period Pemberton evolved into a martinet who had difficult relations with his officers and men.

When the war began, his wife "Pattie," who came from a prominent slave-holding Virginia family, reportedly persuaded him to join the Confederate army. He quickly was promoted to Major General, but during his first major assignment in South Carolina in 1862, stated publicly that Fort Sumter should be abandoned. The enraged governors of South Carolina and Georgia, citing this statement and Pemberton's Northern birth, demanded that he be removed. Jefferson Davis complied by fatefully assigning Pemberton to command of the region around the critically-important city of Vicksburg, Mississippi.

Ulysses Grant's victory at Vicksburg was critical to his rise to command of all Union armies. But for many months in 1862 and 1863 Grant lost thousands of men and spent thousands of dollars in a fruitless effort to take the city. Pemberton successfully fended Grant off for a time. But his poor relationship with subordinates, his failure to comprehend Grant's strategy, and the lack of promised reinforcements ultimately undermined his ability to defend the city. By May 1863 Grant on land and the navy on the river had surrounded the city, and a state of siege ensued. Ultimately, faced with starvation, Pemberton agreed to surrender on July 4. The news of the successful Battle of Gettysburg and the fall of Vicksburg were major morale boosters for the Union.

(Believe is an image of Grant and Pemberton discussing the surrender terms).

HARPER'S PICTORIAL HISTORY OF THE CIVIL WAR. [JULY, 1868.

Davis tried to find a new position for Pemberton, but suspicions about his loyalty were rife in the Confederate army. He was even criticized for surrendering on July 4, Independence Day, thereby giving the Union a propaganda victory. In fact, Pemberton had gotten better conditions for his troops by delaying the agreement, but myths, as always, are more powerful than facts. Ultimately Pemberton was assigned to command the artillery defending Richmond until war's end.

After the war Pemberton farmed in Virginia and then returned to Pennsylvania, where he died in 1881. Even then the question of his wartime "loyalty" stirred emotions, though this time it was from the Union side. Prominent figures, including Pennsylvanian General George Meade, protested against his being buried in his family plot in Laurel Hill cemetery in Philadelphia. Ultimately Pemberton was buried in the cemetery, but in an area away from the family plot.

Further Reading: David M. Smith, *Compelled to Appear in Print: The Vicksburg Manuscript of General John C. Pemberton;* Ironclad Publishing, 2005; Michael B. Ballard, *Pemberton: A Biography*. Jackson: University of Mississippi Press, 1991.

George Pickett and His "Charge"?

George Pickett and the Shad Row

During his Civil War career George Pickett had a moderate record of success, punctuated by several lengthy periods of absence because of wounds or illness. Were it not for two events in which his judgment and abilities came under severe criticism, he would most likely have been considered a relatively-unimportant part of the Confederate war effort.

The first event was the so-called Pickett's Charge on the third day of the Battle of Gettysburg. As in the case of many events of the war, this is a misnomer. Pickett's men were only a part of those who made this famous attack, and he was not in overall command of the troops as they moved forward. The myth that it was solely "Pickett's" charge is, to a significant extent, the result of the work of his widow and her extensive -- and frequently fraudulent -- writing after the war. Further, "Lost Cause" advocates, perhaps fearing that this desperate and wrong-headed attack might be rightfully called "Lee's Fatal Charge" were content to put the onus on Pickett and Longstreet. Pickett, not surprisingly, was extremely angry at Lee for ordering the attack, and their relations were strained for the rest of the war.

The second event, which is less well known but perhaps far more important, was what might be called the "Shad Roe Row." In April 1865 the "Overland Campaign" was nearing its end. Grant had besieged Lee in Richmond and Petersburg for over a year, but the Confederates held out doggedly. Grant decided to try to cut the final supply line into Petersburg and thus force Lee to evacuate both cities. To achieve this objective, he sent a force under General Phil Sheridan to Five Forks, which was on the railroad line.

At the time Pickett was in command of that part of Lee's line. Perhaps not understanding the threat his men were facing, he left the battlefield on April 1 for a fish fry, a Virginia spring tradition of eating shad fish. Pickett was there, behind the lines, when the final and ultimately-successful Union assault began.

When he became aware of the threat, Pickett hurried back, but it was too late. His failure was the proximate cause for Lee's decision to abandon the cities of Richmond and Petersburg and scurry to the west in search of supplies. Two days later a visiting Abraham Lincoln would be sitting at Jefferson Davis's desk in Richmond, the death of the Confederacy only a matter of days away. Soon afterward, Pickett would join Lee in surrender.

(Below is a stylized image of Longstreet and Pickett just before the famous charge)

Further Reading: Lesley J. Gordon, *General George Pickett in Life and Legend,*. Chapel Hill: University of North Carolina Press, 1998; Carol Reardon, *Pickett's Charge in History and Memory*. Chapel Hill: University of North Carolina Press, 1997.

Gen. Pickett taking the order to charge from Gen. Longstreet. Gettysburg, July 3, 1863.

John Pope's Lack of Vision

John Pope at Second Manassas

Pope was chosen to command the Army of Virginia in 1862 in great part because he was an outspoken Republican who had a modest record of success in the West. He was instructed by Secretary of War Stanton to be a troublemaker via critical public statements regarding the reputation of Army of the Potomac commander George McClellan. But he spent much of his first few weeks in command not in preparing his troops, but in being outspoken in public and in Congress.

When in the summer of 1862 he had to face the challenge of Robert E. Lee and Thomas Stonewall Jackson, he again was outspoken about his confidence and judgment. As in the case of his comments to Congress, his failures and defeats made more trouble for him than anything else.

David Strother, one of Pope's staffers, wrote incisively about him, "He is a bright, dashing man, self-confident and clearheaded…but irascible and impulsive in his judgments of men." About Pope at the Second Battle of Manassas, Strother wrote, "In this campaign Pope was entirely deceived and outgeneraled. His own conceit and pride of opinion led him into these mistakes…he was in the general planning of the campaign unable to cope with his opponents."

During Lee's advance, Pope became obsessed with Stonewall Jackson. Failing, as did most Union commanders in that era, to make effective use of his cavalry, Pope rarely knew where Jackson and his division were located. This was especially true when Jackson moved completely around him and ravaged his supplies in the city of Manassas. Pope did finally locate Jackson on August 29 and 30, 1862, in the same area where the First Battle of Manassas had been fought over a year before.

Pope launched attack after attack against Jackson on those days. During this time Pope was told several times, including by senior generals, that Lee and over 15,000 troops were advancing on his left flank after having passed through Thoroughfare Gap (see the historical marker below). Pope, fixated on Jackson, refused to believe them. When Lee did hit his left, Pope finally realized his awful mistake and lack of vision. He and his army were soon on the verge not only of defeat, but also of opening the way to

Washington, 30 miles away. It was only with the help of his subordinates that Pope was able to make an ignominious, yet effective retreat toward Washington.

George McClellan had been ordered to reinforce Pope, but for days he dragged his feet, even as he told his wife that Pope would be defeated. McClellan seldom put the national interest above his own, and this was one of the prime examples since he knew Pope's defeat could lead to greater power for himself.

However, while McClellan's tactics harmed Pope's ability to fight, there is absolutely no question that Pope was primarily responsible for this defeat. He was a poor leader who chose not to rely on subordinates, even those who were capable. He had little or no vision about a battlefield, and he allowed himself to lose focus on the "big picture."

Pope's defeat had significant implications for the war. Lee was now encouraged to take the war to the North, and he invaded Maryland on September 4. The events leading to the Battle of Antietam and, ultimately, the Emancipation Proclamation, were now set in motion.

As for Pope, he was sent to the West to fight Indians, and he was never again called to combat duty during the Civil War. He did remain in the army, but his failure at Second Manassas would always remain the most important event in his life.

Further Reading: Peter Cozzens, *General John Pope, A Life for the Nation*, Champaign: University of Illinois Press, 2000, and John Hennessy, *Return to Bull Run: The Campaign and Battle of Second Manassas.* Norman: University of Oklahoma Press, 2012.

Fitz-John Porter, Political Operative

Fitz-John Porter, Troublemaker Par Excellence

Making trouble for everyone in the army other than his close friend George McClellan seems to have been Porter's stock in trade. That and his inability to control his need to vent openly about his disdain for General John Pope were the keys to his disgraceful cashiering from the army.

Porter was usually an adequate military commander when responsibility fell to him. During the Peninsula campaign he and his men performed well at the Battle of Malvern Hill after McClellan had effectively abandoned the field. Unlike some generals, he also appreciated the potential utility of observation balloons.

Porter was at the same time a skilled political operative, an attribute normally not expected of field generals. He was in constant contact with Democratic newspapermen while McClellan was being criticized by the Lincoln administration. Porter fed information and criticism to the papers for their next editions, and frequently wrote "anonymous" editorials for them.

When Porter criticized Pope before and during the Second Manassas campaign, his messages got into the hands of the Lincoln administration. Pope recommended that Porter be court-martialed for his actions at Second Manassas. The White House complied, but suspended the proceedings for the Maryland campaign. Meanwhile, Secretary of War Stanton planned to stack the deck for Porter's trial.

Porter's conviction was never in doubt, though most historians believe not only that it was a kangaroo court, but also that Porter did not deserve his fate. On the other hand, there is no question that Porter's disdain for Pope led him to shirk his military duties at Second Manassas. Pope was a poor commander and his orders to Porter were often confusing and wrong-headed. But a dynamic Porter, likely would have improved the results for the Union. Porter had no intention of acting in that way, and he paid a price.

(Below is a drawing of his court-martial, with the names of those in attendance written on the figures).

If the Battle of Antietam had been a Union victory, all would likely have been forgiven. But Porter, whose Vth corps was in reserve, did little fighting, and once again his actions played a decisive role. He advised McClellan not to use his corps to support Ambrose Burnside's IXth corps at a critical time of the day. Most historians agree that reinforcing Burnside at that moment would likely have led to Lee's annihilation. Instead the battle was a small Union tactical victory, which nevertheless led to the fateful issuance of the Emancipation Proclamation.

Porter was summarily convicted and cashiered. He spent much of the rest of his life trying to clear his name, and his efforts became embroiled in party politics. Finally, a military board ordered by a Democratic president, Grover Cleveland, removed the conviction from his record. Incongruously and illogically, the board also said that Porter had acted correctly at all times and in the best traditions of the army. The board dismissed his insubordination as a minor issue. Congress eventually restored Porter to the ranks of the army, after which he retired. However the controversies related to this military troublemaker and political operative still stir active debate in Civil War circles.

Further Reading: John Hennessy, *Return to Bull Run: The Campaign and Battle of Second Manassas*. Norman: University of Oklahoma Press, 2012; Stephen Sears, *Landscape Turned Red: The Battle of Antietam*. New York: Ticknor and Fields, 1983; Donald R. Jermann, *Fitz-John Porter: Scapegoat of Second Manassas*. New York: Macfarland, 2008.:

Chapter V: *Uncommon Men, Women and Their Causes*

This group includes some of the most honored and/or well-remembered actors of the Civil War era, a few whose long-term impact, negative and positive, we continue to remember.

Union General **William Tecumseh Sherman**'s (1820-1891) unconventional tactics during and after the Atlanta campaign made him a Union hero and a Confederate *bete noire.*

Union General **Dan Sickles** (1819-1914) was a colorful character who harmed many others in his search for glory and vindication.

Henry Morton Stanley (1841-1904), best known for his Africa explorations, was a soldier on both sides of the Civil War and twice a deserter.

Edwin Stanton (1814-1869) was a superbly-effective Union Secretary of War whose personality and quirks won him well-deserved praise and enmity on many sides.

Harriet Tubman's (1822-1913) flight from slavery and courage rescuing others made her one of the heroes of the era.

Mark Twain's (1835-1910) short time as a Confederate soldier and a deserter are blips on the screen of his overall positive impact on American culture.

Confederate Brigadier **Stand Watie** (1806-1871) was the only American Indian to become a Confederate General Officer, and he was the last Confederate official to formally surrender.

Confederate Private **Sam Watkins**'s (1839-1901) memoir, *Company 'Aytch*, is an unmatched view of the life of a typical "Johnny Reb."

Confederate General **Joseph Wheeler** (1836-1906) was a superb self-promoter whose performance in war, including the Spanish-American war, was mediocre at best.

William Tecumseh Sherman, Warrior

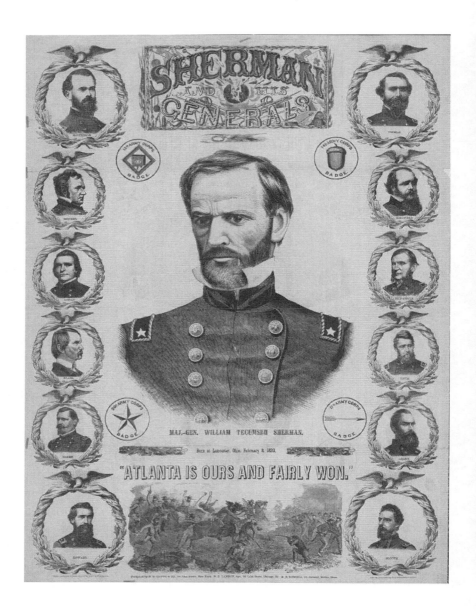

Sherman, the Indirect Method and Hard Hand of War

Sherman and Grant were an effective team, in part because they knew one other's strengths and weaknesses. As Sherman once wrote to Grant, he would always support him because Grant had stood by him when he was crazy and he had stood by Grant when he was drunk. The Battle of Shiloh also seems to have cemented a strong unity between them because their inaction almost resulted in the destruction of their army.

Grant's 1864 orders to Sherman for the so-called "Atlanta Campaign" and for his "March to the Sea" underline that trusting relationship. Before Atlanta Grant directed Sherman, "move against [Joseph] Johnston's army, break it up, and get into the interior of the enemy's country as far as you can, inflicting all the damage you can against their war resources...I leave you free to execute in your own way." Later, having somewhat reluctantly accepted Sherman's justification for his march to the sea, Grant told him, "I say, then, go as you propose." In that order, as with the other, Grant gave Sherman total discretion. Those two campaigns would solidify Sherman's reputation as a trailblazer in military tactics and strategy.

The Atlanta campaign was, for a while, the proverbial "indirect campaign," as described by British military theorist Basil Liddell-Hart. Both Johnston and Sherman had learned that because of advanced artillery and rifle firepower, large-scale infantry frontal attacks against fortified breastworks were no longer advisable. Both sides recognized the power of the defensive, so the campaign's first two months, May and June 1864, consisted of each trying to outflank the other. The only direct attack, by Sherman at Kennesaw Mountain, was an inevitable failure, and Sherman attempted no more such attacks.

Fortunately for Sherman, Johnston was replaced by John Bell Hood, who aggressively attacked the Union forces, even as they set up strong breastworks. He failed each time, suffering far greater losses than the Union side. Ultimately, it was a flanking maneuver by Sherman which successfully completed the campaign by cutting Hood's supply line. The taking of Atlanta helped Union morale and buttressed Lincoln's chances for reelection in 1864.

The "March to the Sea' was innovative in that Sherman cut himself off from his supply line and lived off the land, while bringing the hard hand of war to the South's civilians. As he put it in his immortal comment, "war is cruelty and you cannot refine it." He took the war directly to those who supported the rebel war effort. He reasoned that the Confederate home front was important for keeping the armies in the field, so if there was discontent and devastation there, it would both encourage desertion and worsen morale. He was right.

The hatred of Sherman in some parts of the South because of the actions of some of his troops during the March to the Sea is only partly justified. While his "bummers" (stragglers among the troops who acted on their own) perpetrated abuses, Confederate forces under Joe Wheeler frequently did the same.

(Below is a stylized image of Sherman's March to the Sea).

Further Reading: John F. Marszalek, *Sherman: A Soldier's Passion for Order.* New York: Free Press,1993; W.T. Sherman, *Memoirs of W.T. Sherman.* New York: Appleton, 1873.

Dan Sickles, Superb Self-Promoter

Dan Sickles: Trouble Was His Middle Name

Among those who caused the term "Political General" to be one of disparagement, Dan Sickles was in the front row. His performance at Gettysburg, where he disobeyed orders and almost lost the battle, coupled with his subsequent attempts to blame commanding General George Meade for the results of the battle, are legendary examples of troublemaking and duplicity.

Sickles's well-deserved reputation as a ne'er do-well began in New York City where in the 1840's, as a lawyer, he was accused of financial chicanery. This was not an obstacle – some might say it was an asset – for his rise to a position of influence in New York's Tammany Hall and the Democratic party. He was also a womanizer who often visited ladies of the night, and he married a 16 year old girl, Teresa Bagiolis, whom he had first known when she was an infant.

In 1856, following a tour as a diplomatic secretary of future-president James Buchanan when he was Ambassador to Great Britain, Sickles was elected to Congress. While in office he accomplished very little. But in 1859 he further cemented his reputation when he shot and killed in public a man accused of being his wife's lover. In a sensational trial in which future Secretary of War Edwin Stanton would be one of Sickles's lawyers, he became the first person acquitted in America on the basis of "temporary insanity." (see below for an image of the attack)

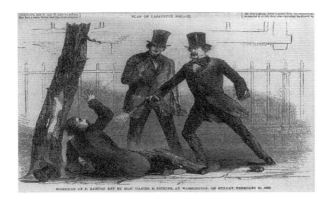

When the Civil War began, Sickles, like many politicians, maneuvered to get a military command. Eventually, he became a brigadier general of volunteers and was part of McClellan's Army of the Potomac in the Peninsula campaign. Later, he became close friends with another general with a shady reputation. Despite Sickles's having been engaged in few battles, Joe Hooker assigned him as commander of the 3rd corps in March 1863 and arranged for him to be promoted to Major General. Sickles performed well at Chancellorsville, but he and General George Meade, 5th corps commander, developed an antipathy for one another soon afterward.

Meade replaced Hooker days before the Battle of Gettysburg. On July 2, Meade placed Sickles's corps at the end of the defensive line. However, Sickles, disobeying orders, moved his troops forward, putting them at significant risk. Meade ordered him to return, but it was too late, and the 3rd corps suffered major casualties. Sickles was wounded, and he would lose a leg as a result.

Sickles was evacuated to Washington where he quickly began spinning tales about his role in the victory at Gettysburg. In Congressional testimony and after the war, he engaged in an active campaign to discredit Meade, lying that the commander had wanted to retreat, but had been dissuaded by his subordinates.

Later, Sickles became active in helping create the Gettysburg battlefield's memorabilia. In a suitable and appropriate capstone to his life, Sickles was removed from the New York State Monuments Commission in 1913 because of suspected theft of its funds. Nevertheless, Sickles received a congressional Medal of Honor and "Sickles Avenue" is part of the Gettysburg Battlefield Park.

Some historians agree with Sickles about the effect of his disobedience of orders at Gettysburg. Sickles claimed that the Confederates were confused by this significant element of a strong Union defensive line moving forward to meet an oncoming attack. Sickles's action, they conjecture, disrupted the Confederates' plans to attack the far left and forced them to focus on the 3rd corps to capture positions which later proved of no value. The debate goes on.

(Below is an image of Gettysburg and Sickles's actions)

Further Reading: James A. Hessler, *Sickles at Gettysburg: The Controversial Civil War General Who Committed Murder, Abandoned Little Round Top, and Declared Himself the Hero of Gettysburg.* Savas-Beatie, 2009; W.A. Swanberg, *Sickles the Incredible.* New York: 1956.

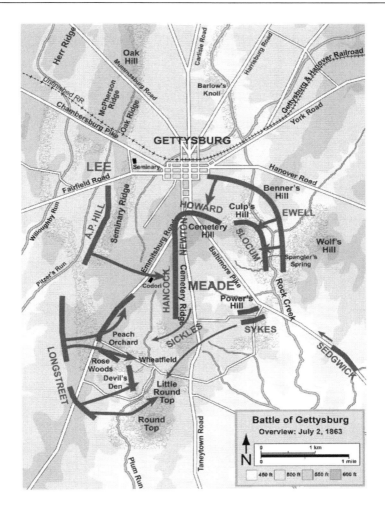

Map by Hal Jespersen, www.cwmaps.com

Henry Stanley on Three Continents

Henry Stanley, Prisoner, Deserter, Explorer

Before he met Dr. Livingstone in 1871 in Africa and allegedly uttered those timeless words, "Dr. Livingstone, I presume," Henry Morton Stanley had established an unenviable record in the United States during the Civil War. That record and that of his other actions are recorded in Stanley's autobiography, *The Autobiography of Sir Henry Morton Stanley,* much of which modern historians have determined to be fallacious.

Stanley did join the Confederate army and fight at the Battle of Shiloh, after which he was taken prisoner. While in a Union prison, he agreed to become a "Galvanized Yankee," joining the Union army. Not long afterward he deserted, and after service on merchant ships, joined the Union navy. He deserted from the Navy in early 1865. As a result, he was not only one of the few individuals to have served in both armies and the Union navy, but also to have done so as a non-citizen! It is debatable whether these events qualify him for being a trailblazer or a troublemaker, or both.

Stanley's real name was John Rowlands, an Englishman who, after being orphaned at 18, moved to New Orleans in 1859. When the war began, having taken the name of his employer, Stanley enlisted in the 6th Arkansas Infantry. Given his shallow patriotism, it perhaps is not surprising that he willingly joined the Union army, especially since he would no longer be in prison. Some sources state that he deserted from the army. In neither case did he do any fighting. Nor did he engage in any military action during his Navy "career."

After his final desertion, Stanley launched a successful career as a trailblazing journalist and explorer. His trip to find Livingstone was only one of his many adventures. Those included searching for the source of the Nile and claiming what would become the Belgian Congo for the King of Belgium. He was knighted by Queen Victoria in 1899 for his service to the British Empire.

(Below is a stylized drawing of the meeting of Stanley and Livingstone. Note the American flag being carried by Stanley's assistant):

Further Reading: John Bierman, *Dark Safari: The Life Behind the Legend of Henry Morton Stanley*. Austin: University of Texas Press, 1993; Martin Dugard, et.al., *Into Africa The Epic Adventures of Stanley and Livingstone*. New York: Doubleday, 2003.

Edwin Stanton, Political Chameleon

Edwin Stanton Plays Uriah Heep

The Union's second and extremely-effective Secretary of War was a prickly and pugnacious man who tended to act impulsively. But he was in every way a trailblazer in using this position for effective leadership in war. People tended to hate him or love him, and there was often little common ground. The two biographies of Stanton noted below are prime examples of how history has judged him: Marvel's book is a nearly-endless series of condemnations of his actions; Stahr's emphasizes his many accomplishments and gives short shrift to his personality quirks.

Esteemed Civil War historian James McPherson has written, "in Edwin Stanton and Montgomery Meigs, aided by the entrepreneurial talent of northern businessmen, the Union developed superior managerial talent to mobilize and organize the North's greater resources for victory in the modern industrialized conflict that the Civil War became." (*Battle Cry of Freedom*). But whereas that talent was obvious in Meigs, who already had a reputation as a skilled engineer and manager, Stanton came to the job with no particularly-relevant talent.

He had been Buchanan's Attorney General and was well known in Washington as a skilled and crafty lawyer, yet someone slippery enough to keep Dan Sickles from being convicted for an obvious murder. Stanton was a Unionist Democrat who had been displeased at Buchanan's dilatory actions during the secession crisis. When Simon Cameron, Lincoln's first Secretary of War, proved both corrupt and inadequate, Lincoln appointed Stanton.

Establishing solid relations with Lincoln, Meigs, and congressional leaders, Stanton put into effect efficient supply and transportation methods for the army. He also established, at first, a close relationship with George McClellan, a fellow Democrat, when the latter was General-in-Chief early in the war. In each of these relationships, Stanton was skilled at playing up to them in person while at the same time disdaining them in private.

Stanton's split with McClellan because of his inaction during the Peninsular campaign was exacerbated when Stanton ceased recruiting volunteers on the presumption of an early Union victory. Later, his and

Lincoln's decision to change strategy and not send reinforcements to McClellan made the latter Stanton's bitter enemy. Stanton's support for John Pope sealed the deal.

Like everyone else in the Cabinet, Stanton opposed giving command to McClellan for the Maryland campaign, and he adamantly pushed for his removal after McClellan failed to follow up after Antietam. Stanton was equally unhappy with McClellan's successors, Burnside, Hooker, and Meade. He criticized the latter after his victory at Gettysburg for not following up and destroying Lee thereafter.

Stanton was equally critical of Union generals in the West until the emergence of Grant and Sherman. After Rosecrans's defeat at Chickamauga, Stanton lobbied hard for his removal from command. Ironically, Stanton later pushed hard for the replacement of George Thomas, who had succeeded Rosecrans, for his slow movements before his victory at the Battle of Nashville in December 1864..

When Grant became General-in-Chief, Stanton's role became less central to decision-making, though his decision to allow absentee voting by soldiers played a key role in Lincoln's re-election. Stanton later chastised Lincoln when the latter, visiting Richmond, agreed to allow the Virginia legislature to re-convene; Lincoln then reversed this ill-advised decision.

A final example of Stanton's strange personality came when he disapproved Sherman's initial surrender agreement with Johnston. Instead of keeping the issue secret, Stanton published Sherman's proposal and ordered Chief of Staff Halleck to announce that Sherman's orders should not be followed. An insulted Sherman refused to shake Stanton's hand at the Grand Review of the troops in May 1865. .

Stanton's prickly relationship with Andrew Johnson eventually led to the latter's impeachment when he tried to remove Stanton from office. Though Johnson was not convicted and remained in office, he agreed to cease interfering with military reconstruction. With Grant about to become President in 1869, Stanton resigned, his work done.

(Below is a contemporary image of Lincoln, Stanton, and others "breaking the backbone" of the rebellion):

Further Reading: William Marvel, *Lincoln's Autocrat: The Life of Edwin Stanton.* Chapel Hill: University of North Carolina Press, 2015; Walter Stahr, *Stanton: Lincoln's War Secretary.* New York: Simon and Schuster, 2017.

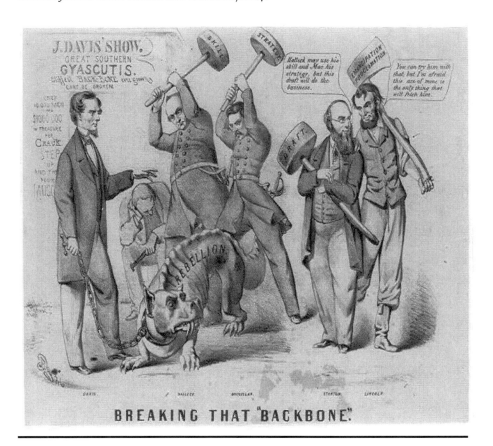

Harriet Tubman, Hero

Harriet Tubman and Emancipation

The recent controversy over whether Harriet Tubman should appear on a $20 bill to replace President Andrew Jackson brought "re-fighting the Civil War" once again onto the public stage. Whether or not that change ever takes place, Harriet Tubman's trailblazing greatness as a champion of egalitarianism is not controversial.

Tubman's fame began with her activities in the 1840's and 1850's as an escapee from slavery in Maryland and as a rescuer of many others with the assistance of participants in the Underground Railroad. She became well-known in abolitionist circles during this period, and she even considered going along with John Brown on his ill-fated raid into Harpers Ferry in 1859.

During the Civil War she worked in Port Royal, South Carolina caring for and nursing black fugitives. She also acted as a spy and a scout for Union soldiers. In 1863 she reportedly was the first woman to lead a military assault by Union troops against a Confederate outpost in South Carolina. She also supported the 54th Massachusetts "Colored Troops" who made the famous attack on Fort Wagner which was immortalized in the movie, *Glory*.

After the war Tubman was active in lobbying for both blacks' and women's rights. Published books about her life and activities, as well as her receiving, after a great deal of lobbying, a Civil War pension, provided her financial support. She died in 1913 and was recognized even then as one of the major figures in American history.

Tubman today is memorialized by the National Park Service's *Harriet Tubman Underground Railroad National Historic Park* in Maryland and the *Harriet Tubman National Historic Park* in New York. An image of the first is below:

Further Reading: Kate Clifford Larson, *Bound for the Promised Land: Harriet Tubman, Portrait of an American Hero*. New York: Ballantine, 2003; Milton Sernett, *Harriet Tubman: Myth, Memory, and History*. Durham: Duke University Press, 2007.

Mark Twain, Reluctant Soldier

Mark Twain and Grant, A Key Friendship

To say that Samuel Clemens/Mark Twain was both a trailblazer and a troublemaker is a significant understatement. His books have entertained generations of Americans both because of his unique portrayals of every day life and because of his superb sense of humor. But Twain often made trouble by breaking taboos and revealing uncomfortable elements of life.

Twain's short, uneventful Civil War military activity consisted of two weeks service in the Confederate army (the Missouri militia), which he fictionalized in the short story, *The Private History of a Campaign that Failed.* He and some friends had apparently joined the militia on a lark, and after a couple of weeks of boredom, like tens of thousands of others, he deserted his post. He went west to work for his brother Orion, who was Secretary of the Nevada Territory. Soon afterward he launched his successful career as a writer, spending the war far from the fighting. Twain wrote several versions of his "military experience," once joking that once he had almost had to fight against Grant while both were in Missouri.

Twain's later relationship with Grant came towards the end of the former's public life and at the height of Twain's fame. Between 1865 and 1884 Twain wrote many of his most famous works, including *Huckleberry Finn, Tom Sawyer,* and *Life on the Mississippi*, and he amassed a fortune. However, eventually he would lose everything, declaring bankruptcy in 1894.

During the early 1880's Twain heard about the plight of Grant, who had been left penniless because of his business failures and who was suffering with what would be a terminal case of throat cancer. In order to provide for his family, Grant began writing his *Memoirs* in 1884, and they were completed just a few days before his death the next year. Twain, who had created his own publishing company, agreed to publish the book, which was a critical and financial success. Twain marketed the book effectively, and he sold over 350,000 sets, ensuring the financial strength of the Grant family..

Twain's writings about the Civil War itself were few. But his commentaries about race and slavery and how those issues divided the nation are among the best in all of American literature. In what some call the greatest American novel, the relationship between Huckleberry Finn and his enslaved friend Jim starkly provide the reader with the essence of prewar racial divisions in American society. That book and his contribution to the history of the war via his publishing of Grant's memoirs are essential elements of Twain's Civil War legacy as a trailblazer – and a troublemaker too.

(Below is an image of Grant in his last days, writing his memoirs).

Further Reading: Joe B. Fulton, *The Reconstruction of Mark Twain: How a Confederate Bushwhacker Became the Lincoln of our Literature.* Baton Rouge: LSU Press, 2011; Mark Perry, *Grant and Twain: The Story of a Friendship that Changed America.* Random House, 2004; Chris Mackowski and Kristopher White, *Grant's Last Battle: The Story Behind the Personal Memoirs of Ulysses S. Grant.* Savis-Beatie, 2019.

Stand Watie, Cherokee Confederate General

Stand Watie and His Last Stand

The history of American Indians during the Civil War is as varied as the number and life styles of the tribes. Some groups allied with the Union or the Confederacy. Some were internally-divided and also switched allegiances periodically. Others tried to avoid the conflict completely. But all, in the end, would fall victim to the tide of history, which the war would only accelerate.

Stand Watie (loosely translated as "stand firm") was a slave-holding, plantation-owning Cherokee chief in "Indian Territory" (Oklahoma) when the Civil War began. His tribe opted to support the Confederacy, in part because the potential creation of a state by a Republican-led federal government might, they feared, reduce their autonomy. Watie organized the 1st Cherokee Mounted Rifles cavalry regiment in 1861 and was appointed its Colonel. They fought in the Battle of Pea Ridge, March 6-8 1862, while also engaging in fighting with other Indian factions. In 1862 Watie became the Principal Chief of the Cherokees.

Watie was promoted to brigadier general in the Confederate army in 1864, and his First Indian Brigade fought in several battles in the trans-Mississippi region. They also fought against other Cherokee, most of whom had supported the Union. On June 23, 1865, Watie became the last Confederate general to surrender. Later, given his prominence in his tribe, he became a member of the Indian "Southern Treaties Commission" which negotiated the postwar Indian treaties for the Cherokee.

(Below is an image of President Andrew Johnson greeting some of the Indian delegations in 1867):

Further Reading: Laurence Hauptman, *Between Two Fires: American Indians in the Civil War*. New York: Free Press, 1995; Clarissa Confer, *The Cherokee Nation in the Civil War*. Norman: University of Oklahoma Press, 2007.

Sam Watkins, Infantryman

"Co. Aytch": Maury Grays, First Tennessee Regiment, Or, a Side Show of the Big Show

R. Sam Watkins

Sam Watkins and the Meaning of War

Sam Watkins's trailblazing memoir of his life as an enlisted man in the Confederate Army of Tennessee was not written until the 1880's; and some have questioned the complete accuracy of the book. Even so, *Company 'Aytch* remains one of the best memoirs of the war from the viewpoint of the foot soldier.

Sam was born into a relatively-prosperous family in Mount Pleasant, Tennessee, and he was 21 when the Civil War began. In the first section of his book, he set the tone of his memoir by comparing the early enthusiasm for war with its realities. He wrote, "we soon found that the glory of war was at home among the ladies and not upon the field of blood and carnage of death, where our colleagues were mutilated and torn by shot and shell."

Watkins would ultimately join the Army of Tennessee, which was the major fighting force in the West for the Confederacy from late 1862 on. While he did not rise above the rank of Corporal, he could be called the ultimate survivor. He fought at most of his Army's major battles, including Shiloh, Perryville, Chickamauga, Atlanta campaign, Franklin, and Nashville. When Joe Johnston surrendered to Sherman in North Carolina in April 1865, Sam was one of only seven soldiers remaining who had served in the Army of Tennessee during its entire existence.

Watkins's pithy commentaries in his book about his commanding generals, all of whom he supported, but not all of whom he admired, are particularly noteworthy:

Braxton Bragg: "Bragg was a good disciplinarian, and if he had cultivated the love and respect of his troops...the results would have been different. Bragg was the great autocrat...He loved to crush the spirit of his men."

Joseph Johnston: "When the news came, like pouring oil over troubled waters, that General Joe E. Johnston, of Virginia, had taken command of the Army of Tennessee, men returned to their companies, order was restored. ..Such a man was Joseph E. Johnston...We privates loved you because you made us love ourselves."

John Bell Hood: "The most terrible and disastrous blow that the South ever received was when Hon. Jefferson Davis placed Hood in command of the Army of Tennessee. I saw, I will say, thousands of men cry like babies."

One final quote underlines Watkins's quirky yet realistic view of war: "I always shot at privates. It was they that did the shooting and killing, and if I could kill or wound a private, why, my chances were so much better."

(Below is an image of Johnston's surrender to Sherman):

Further Reading: Sam Watkins, *Company "Aytch": The First Tennessee Regiment or a Side Show to the Big Show.* Cumberland Presbyterian Publishing House, 1882; Steven Woodworth, *Jefferson Davis and His Generals: The Failure of Confederate Command in the West.* Lawrence: University Press of Kansas, 1990; Bell Wiley, *The Life of Johnny Reb: The Common Soldier of the Confederacy.* Baton Rouge: LSU Press, 1943

Joe Wheeler, Cavalryman

"Fighting" Joe Wheeler

Unlike his Union nickname-namesake, "Fighting Joe Hooker," Confederate General Joseph Wheeler relished that nickname. He exemplified it during three separate wars: Civil War; Spanish-American War; and Philippine-American War. He also served for several terms in the House of Representatives and, in part because of his skillful self-promotion, he is one of Alabama's representative statues in Congress's Statuary Hall.

Wheeler's biographer notes that he was a controversial Civil War figure about whom most historians have expressed negative judgments. He wrote that when he told a leading historian of his intention to write this biography, the historian "wrote me to complain that Wheeler was perhaps the most overrated of the Confederate generals and to express the hope that I would 'give the little son of a bitch what he deserves.'" (Longacre, Preface). Presumably that historian thought Wheeler was more of a troublemaker than a trailblazer.

Wheeler graduated from West Point in 1859 and was trained at the cavalry school in Pennsylvania before deciding to join the Confederacy. The fact that he became the cavalry commander of the Army of Tennessee when he was only 25 was a cause of his friction with older, more seasoned commanders, especially Nathan Bedford Forrest. After a particularly-difficult contretemps in early 1863, Forrest allegedly told Wheeler, "Tell General Bragg [Army of Tennessee commander] that I will be in my coffin before I will fight again under your command."

Wheeler effectively used his cavalry forces on raids against Union railroads and as a shield for both advances and retreats by Confederate forces. After the 1864 Atlanta campaign, he was sent by John Bell Hood to cut Sherman's supply line back to Chattanooga, but he was unsuccessful. Wheeler and his cavalry were subsequently the only organized resistance to Sherman's "March to the Sea," but he could only harass the much larger force, to little effect. Also, it appears that Wheeler occasionally lost control of some of his men, whom Southern newspapers at the time charged with "destructive lawlessness." When Wheeler was sent to protect Jefferson Davis's escape in 1865, he was captured and imprisoned for two months before being paroled.

Although aged 61 when the Spanish-American War began, Wheeler volunteered to serve and became a Major General of Volunteers. He was active in fighting the Spanish forces in Cuba, and then sailed to the Philippines to help put down that insurrection. In 1900 he was given a commission as a Brigadier General in the United States regular army. As a result, one could say he was "thrice a patriot," for the United States; for the Confederacy; and then again for the United States.

After his death Wheeler received many honors in addition to being memorialized in statuary hall. Several facilities in Alabama are named after him, and the U.S. Navy named a World War II liberty ship after him. He is one of the few Confederates buried in Arlington Cemetery.

(Below is a picture of Wheeler (bearded) with Teddy Roosevelt and General Leonard Wood, in Tampa, Florida before going to Cuba).

Further Reading: Edward G. Longacre, *A Soldier to the Last: Major General Joseph Wheeler in Blue and Gray.* Washington: Potomac Books, 2006; John and David Eicher, *Civil War High Commands.* Stanford: Stanford University Press, 2001.

Chapter VI: *The 50th Trailblazer: A Collective View*

The late-15th century morality play *Everyman*, author unknown, follows the title character's search for truth and an understanding of good and evil. The play concludes with his realization that in the end it is only his good deeds which should accompany him as he faces God at the last judgment.

Few in the Civil War era likely read *Everyman*. But the tens of thousands of mostly-anonymous EveryMan and EveryWoman who participated in the war presumably did so believing they were performing good deeds. The combatants – soldiers and sailors – and the non-combatants – soldiers' wives, nurses, telegraphers, drummer boys, chaplains, cooks, *vivandieres* (camp sutlers, who also performed other helpful tasks), etc. -- all played an important role in the war. So in their own way, each of them was a trailblazer.

Because they are anonymous, we know little about them. However, we can see some of them and understand a bit about them by viewing the Library of Congress's photos below. Collectively, these men and women are the 50th member of the group, *Civil War Trailblazers*.

COMBATANTS

The Grand Review of Soldiers, May 23, 1865, Washington

1. *Typical soldiers*

205

2. U.S. "Colored" Troops

3. *Union Indian Soldiers*

207

4. Soldiers with their wives

5. *Sailors*

210

NON-COMBATANTS

"Nuns of the Battlefield" Memorial, Washington, DC

1. Nurses

THE LETTER FOR HOME

THE SISTER OF CHARITY

2. Telegraphers

3. Drummer Boys

215

4. Chaplains

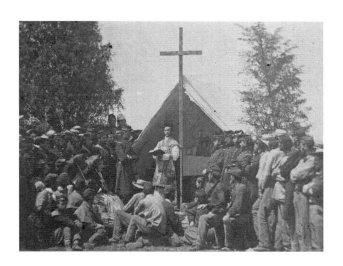

5. Cooks

WHAT DO I WANT, JOHN HENRY?

6. Vivandieres

7. Signal Corpsmen

8. Musicians/Bands

Band of 107th U.S. Colored Infantry

220

9. Baggage Train Drivers/Cattle Drovers

Readers are welcome and encouraged to review this book on amazon.com and other social media, especially Facebook and Instagram. Please also feel free to contact me via my personal web-site:

https://civilwarhistory-geneschmiel.com

and my amazon.com author page,
https://www.amazon.com/-/e/B00HV4SSWK .

GENE SCHMIEL has written and lectured about the Civil War since the publication by Ohio University Press in 2014 of his award-winning biography, *Citizen-General: Jacob Dolson Cox and the Civil War Era.* His second and third books, *Lincoln, Antietam, and a Northern Lost Cause*, and *Ohio Heroes of the Battle of Franklin,* were published in 2019. He holds a Ph.D. degree in History from The Ohio State University and has taught at four universities. For 24 years he was a U.S. Department of State Foreign Service Officer. The images is of Schmiel sitting in his home office, a copy of Jacob Cox's *Military Reminiscences of the Civil War,* open in front of him.

Made in the USA
Middletown, DE
29 April 2024

53552441R00139